Franklinstein

Or, the making of a modern neighborhood

Franklinstein

Or, the making of a modern neighborhood

Susan Landers

2.11.16

Thanks for coming to
the San Diego debut!

ROOF BOOKS
NEW YORK

ISBN: 978-1-931824-64-4
Library of Congress Control Number: 2016931265

Cover art by Ann Landers Beatus
Author photo by Natasha Dwyer

 This book is made possible, in part, by the New York
State Council on the Arts with the support of
Governor Andrew Cuomo and the New York State Legislature.

Roof Books
are published by
Segue Foundation
300 Bowery, New York, NY 10012
seguefoundation.com

Roof Books
are distributed by
Small Press Distribution
1341 Seventh Street
Berkeley, CA. 94710-1403
800-869-7553 or spdbooks.org

In memory of my parents,
Jeanne and Art

*I shall relate events that impressed me with feelings
which, from what I had been, have made me what I am.*
—Mary Shelley

*Your history is so remarkable, that if you do not give it,
someone else will certainly give it.*
—Benjamin Franklin

*It is a very difficult thing to have courage
for that which no one is thinking is a serious thing.*
—Gertrude Stein

There is a here here.
—Ed Feldman, Germantown resident

Contents

BEFORE I BEGAN TO FORM THE FULL SENTENCES

I wrote a dialogue.
—Benjamin Franklin

Everything he is ever doing is a thing he can be boasting.
—Gertrude Stein

SCENE 1

FRANKLIN: What good shall I do this day?
STEIN: A little each day to be written.
FRANKLIN: By constant labor.
STEIN: Beginning of a struggling to resist a beginning
of an ending.
FRANKLIN: I took a fancy to poetry.
STEIN: The living that she had always had inside her.
FRANKLIN: Writing little pieces.
STEIN: Always they are us and we them.
FRANKLIN: Like so many ants.
STEIN: So many lives in this one living.

SCENE 2

STEIN: I would tell it then to almost anyone
who would listen.
FRANKLIN: My first project of a public nature.
STEIN: Writing for myself and strangers.
FRANKLIN: To make that recollection as durable as possible by
putting it down in writing.
STEIN: From the memory of the impression of them
and then there will be a reconstruction.
FRANKLIN: It is not likely that anyone beside yourself can
sufficiently master the facts of your life.

STEIN: To be a master to them.

FRANKLIN: My hopes of success were founded on this.

SCENE 3

STEIN: Sometimes then I think it is all foolishness this
           I am writing.

FRANKLIN: Good people will cease efforts deemed to be hopeless.

STEIN: There was just enough concentration in her to keep
           her from failure.

FRANKLIN: Being connected in my mind with a great and
           extensive project.

STEIN: A little writing of the telling of the knowing.

FRANKLIN: Cut like a thread into several pieces.

STEIN: Repeating coming out of them makes a history.

FRANKLIN: A beautiful regularity, the streets.

PROLOGUE

IT WAS MY DESIGN TO EXPLAIN (PART 1)

At the beginning of this writing I was reading. Reading two books I had never read before: *The Autobiography of Benjamin Franklin* and *The Making of Americans*. And as I was reading, I thought: I should make a new book. A new book from pieces. A new book using only Ben's words and Gertrude's. And so I did that. For months. Cutting and pasting little pieces. To make a monster. And it was so boring.

It was so boring, my dead thing of parts.

Then the church I grew up in closed. The church where my mother and father were married. The church where they baptized their babies. A church in Philadelphia in the neighborhood where I grew up. A kind of rundown place. A place of row homes and vacants and schist.

And when I went there to see that place—the place that was with me from my very beginning—I thought, this will breathe life into my pieces. This will be the soul of my parts. I thought: if I could write the story of this place and its beginnings, this writing would be the right thing, a kind of living.

This is where my writing began.

At the beginning of this writing, historian David Young told me there is Germantown the place—a place of demographics, statistics, boundaries—and Germantown the constructed historical place—what people have chosen to save and memorialize, ignore or forget—and how some of those who talk about its history are plagued by nostalgia, by notions of an idealized past that never existed. He warned me that strong personal connections to this place can intensify a sense of decline, and that this melancholy does little to interpret the past in ways that do justice to the neighborhood as it exists today.

address the problem

17

This is where my writing began: in a church I felt compelled to visit before it closed, before it became another vacant, beautiful building in a neighborhood of vacant, beautiful buildings. At the beginning of this writing, I was participating in behavior long practiced in Germantown—that of white people mourning what was.

*

Whenever I think about the church whose closing was the beginning of this writing, the church that brought me back to the neighborhood after so many years away, the first thing I picture is stained glass. The church had the most unusual stained glass windows—medieval in their complexity and color, and modern in their subject. The windows were made by an Irishman and depicted his ancestors, a congregation of Irish saints.

The glassmaker, a man named Sharkey, raised his family in the neighborhood. My parents knew his son, who would go on to become a stained glassmaker and teach others the craft. Sharkey's son taught the man who removed the windows from the church after it closed. That man works in a studio just a few blocks away from the church, in an unmarked garage at the end of an alley.

The alley, which runs behind the house I grew up in, runs alongside an old friend's house. That boy, named Larry, became a friend after he told a group of boys to chase me past the unmarked garage so that he could "save" me at the corner of Keyser Street. Once, he had a birthday party and his mother let me win at musical chairs.

Often, his house smelled like ether. Later, his family moved away, and the abandoned house took on a moldy, pissy, brick smell. I never went back inside, but for years I stared at it from my bedroom window, where I would sit reading on the radiator.

Some attachments to place feel like sadness.

When I first heard about the church's closing, I felt a sadness I couldn't put into words, which I thought would be quelled, or maybe intensified, by visiting the church one last time. I hadn't been back in the neighborhood in nearly a decade, the last time was when my siblings moved our mother into a senior care facility after she broke her hip falling down the stairs. Little did my mother know that after she dragged herself to the little black box of a phone on the wall to call for help, she would never return to her home of fifty years again.

When I visited the house shortly before its new owner moved in, I was struck by how little was in it. Never one to keep or buy things she didn't need, my mother had been shedding the house of its stuff for years. This made finding a memento to take from the house difficult, and I found myself keeping things I might have otherwise forgotten: aluminum measuring spoons, an egg beater, the cast iron doorstop that came with the house when my parents bought it in 1957.

Things of another time.

Several years after that visit, the church announced its closure. By that time, the number of parishioners had dwindled to about a dozen, so few that they held Mass each Sunday in a room in the rectory. The church's two sanctuaries—a modern basement chapel where I went to Mass as a child, and the upper church capable of seating nearly a thousand—were both too big for the current congregation.

When some of the former parishioners heard about the church's clos-ing, they expressed their grief on Facebook. Many had been part of the area's "white flight" in the 1960s and '70s. When the pastor de-cided to hold the church's final Mass in the basement chapel—the sanctuary his current parishioners felt a stronger attachment to—some former parishioners complained. They insisted that the pastor hold the last Mass in the upper church, a site that loomed large in their memory. They promised to bring so many people back for the service that there'd be no way they could fit anywhere else.

Some attachments to place feel like ownership.

So many former parishioners did, in fact, show up for the last Mass that it was held in the upper church. One man arranged for school buses to bring former parishioners from a parking lot a couple miles away, a parking lot where, he explained, it would be safe to park your car.

After Mass, I met the man who arranged for the buses. We stood in the church's empty parking lot. He was staring at the surrounding houses and shaking his head. He said to me—this man who moved away before I was born—before I was brought home to live where so many others are currently living—he said to me, this used to be a great place to raise a family.

Some attachments to place are fraught with code.

In his history of Detroit, Thomas Sugrue writes: "As the city's racial demography changed…white neighborhood organizations acted to define and defend the invisible boundaries that divided the city. Their actions were, in large part, an attempt to mark their territory symbolically and visibly, to stake out turf and remind outsiders that to violate those borders was to risk grave danger."

After the church's closing, when I visited the stained glass studio nearby, where artisans restore windows from churches that have closed, I found a map of Philadelphia's Irish-Catholic parishes from 1949. Each parish was demarcated by lines and labeled by name. Within some parishes, additional Catholic churches appeared, represented by symbols. In the legend, under the heading "Other," these churches were listed by name and by the congregation's race/ethnicity, for instance, "St. Michael of the Saints (Italian)" or "St. Catherine of Sienna (colored)."

To be a part of something larger than oneself.

*

In 1983, Germantown celebrated the 300th anniversary of its "founding" by German settlers. For ten thousand years before the Germans arrived, the Lenni-Lenape lived in the area. The Lenni-Lenape cut a great road through the city—what became Germantown Avenue—said to have been covered in oyster shells before being paved with Belgian blocks and trolley tracks.

To celebrate their ancestors' arrival at a place where others had already been living, representatives from Germany paraded down Germantown Avenue wearing Prussian uniforms and carrying rifles. Expecting to find a quaint historic village, the Germans were dismayed by the sight of litter, graffiti, and vacant buildings. They were surprised by the neighborhood's lack of "German-ness." They called it a "black forest."

I don't remember seeing Prussians, but I do recall becoming interested in the neighborhood's historic houses around this time. They were such pretty houses—standalone, with wooden shutters and marble steps or iron posts to hold a horse. They were houses that seemed to mean something to history, deemed worthy of preserving, so that summer I walked up and down Germantown Avenue and lifted their knockers to see if anyone was home.

I remember a caretaker at Grumblethorpe pointing to a brown spot on the floor and saying it was the blood of a British soldier. The soldier had died there after getting shot in a cemetery down the street, a small burial ground up the hill from the church that had closed, a cemetery I had never visited until the beginning of this writing.

 For as long as I had known it, the cemetery had been chained up, full of trash, and creepy not for its dead, but for the possibility of its living. Some of its markers pre-date the Revolutionary War. Many bear familiar names, like Benezet, a nearby street and a man who appears in *The Autobiography of Benjamin Franklin*, or Keyser, a street at the end of an alley, or Nice, the family for whom Nicetown is named, the neighborhood down the hill, across the tracks, on the other side of Wayne Junction.

Between every one then some kind of connection.

When I visited the church at the time of its closing, the cemetery happened to be open to visitors. A guide told me the last shot of the Battle of Germantown was taken there, a battle we—the people, the revolutionaries—lost, but which was still considered a turning point in the war.

The point our enemies came to see who they were truly up against.

In the 1960s, an urban renewal plan led to what some call the second battle of Germantown. The plan included tearing down houses and installing a multi-lane roadway, a bypass, near the neighborhood's commercial strip. Planners described their approach as "condemning in order to restore."

Its proponents were largely non-residents with business interests in the neighborhood. Opposition was driven by a loose coalition of community members, neighbors who wanted renewal efforts to focus on the needs of the area's vulnerable residents. Their opposition increased after it became clear that the planners did not want community input. As one planner put it: "You can't be democratic and get things done." After years of arguing, the city struck down the plan. No new plan was developed in its place.

Nearly everyone I talked to about the neighborhood mentions the department stores—sometimes out of nostalgia and sometimes out of frustration over the paucity of commercial services. When I lived there, the larger stores had mostly closed, but the neighborhood still had a fairly active commercial strip, with a Blockbuster, the Payless, and several small local banks. Today, in place of the stores I remember, are charter schools. One named Imani, or the belief in a people and the righteousness of struggle. Another named Mastery, part of a chain. And one named for a Revolutionary War general, General "Mad Anthony" Wayne. As I was ending this writing, Imani announced its closure.

*

In the beginning of this writing I thought: I must make alive the feeling of importance these little lost gentle things hold, existence being not very strong in them.

Some connections to place are patronizing.

23

In the beginning of this writing, I thought of this place as a lost place, a place I could find on the internet, starting with a little drugstore on a corner, a building at the corner of a street named for no one and an avenue named after a general named Wayne. Now vacant, the corner drugstore was where I had my first under-the-table job at 14, counting out pills with a little spatula and a tray. Illegally working in a legal drug trade.

So many pretty little valiums and their little
cutout hearts.
Little windows into little worlds.

In the beginning of this writing, I stared into a screen and its little windows at what had become a vacant drugstore. In one window, I found a record that suggested the pharmacist I used to work for still owned the building. In another window, a record said the pharmacist left the building in care of someone else. In another, a record suggested the man taking care of the building might be the same man who was arrested for selling drugs outside it. And that man had the same name of a boy I grew up with, a boy I don't remember anything about except that he scared me.

In the beginning of this writing, drawing connections between records and feelings and names found in little windows on the internet drew a charge. And I thought that in drawing these connections, these sparks, between records and feelings and names, that I could bring forth a life of this place and its history.

" Frankinstien"

24

But those sparks were without grace and harsh.

To come closer

to come to see

this writing must meander.

Part One: Pieces

so now then we begin again this history of us

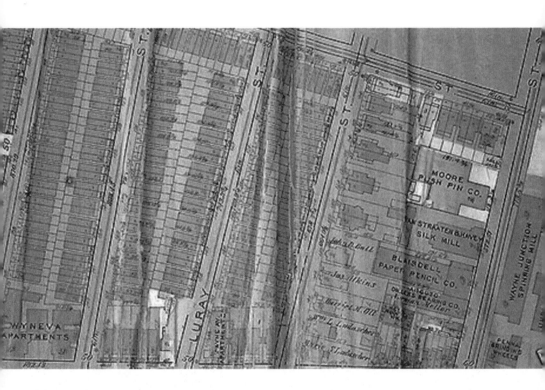

IT HAS A PLACE FOR ME AS LIVING

A place about which some has been written
and some has been not, and people
have very strong feelings.
→ A place of good blocks and bad blocks and brick roads ←
and boxwoods. The site
of America's first gingko tree.
The birthplace of pushpins and Louisa May Alcott.
A place of sparrows and spires and schist.
Where the Lenni-Lenape cut a road.
Where a battle was lost and Washington lived.
Where Still kept his records of the Underground Railroad.
Where white people sought refuge from fever.
Where black people sought refuge from Jim Crow.
Where the Irish and Italians built separate churches.
Where mill workers worked, where workers took trains,
and families like birds came and went.
Where addicts stole drainpipes for copper for crack.
Where someone once told me I couldn't be from.
A place of train tracks and plane trees and vacants and trolleys.
Where people make history and witness or forget—
                    or forget and re-write or make history.

IT IS HARD LIVING DOWN THE TEMPERS
WE ARE BORN WITH

> *It was a dark and stormy day, and then a burst of*
> *sunshine came into our world.*
> —My mother, on my origin story

They brought me—the eighth baby—they brought me home—
like the seven other babies before me—to a rowhouse
in Germantown.
Where my father was born—where my mother was born—
where they were born and had histories and made babies.

And this is a history of some of them.

This will come out slowly as it is written down about them.

My mother was the fourth baby—the fourth baby born
in a house on Milne Street—before Milne Street was a street,
it was a parcel—a parcel of land with an abandoned mansion—
a mansion abandoned by Milne—a man with a mill
and a mansion the latter of which he abandoned
because the mill near his mansion disgusted him.

—And that was 1908.

This is part of the history of this place and its people—
how they were always beginning—how they
were always changing—how they were always forgetting
and remembering they were beginning and changing.

But in the meantime—

The builder wanted to build houses on what would become
Milne Street—and this shocked the politicians
who called the land worthless—worthless land near a mill
and a railway—except to a builder and a buyer
and my mother was born there
in the house the builder built on Milne Street.

                                        —And that was 1927.

One who doesn't have it in them to feel as big as any world
may begin a story with a house on Milne Street
                —in a house called an airlite—
where the kitchen and the dining room share a space in the back.

Not a shotgun or a railroad but a rowhouse nonetheless.

One may begin a story with a house on Milne Street—
because stories begin everywhere—even on streets
not named for anyone—to a street not named for anyone,
                        as far as I can tell, I was brought
—to a house not an airlite but a rowhouse nonetheless—
I was brought to the house where a phone rang
—and I lived there till I didn't in the house not an airlite
        but a shotgun or a railroad—with the others.

                        And that was 1971.

It has a place for me as living.

Working hard to be one telling someone something.

This is the way I feel about me writing.

This is the way I feel about Ben Franklin:
Ben Franklin is full of street names.
Logan, Morris, Penn.

Men turning men into streets.

Always they are us and we them.

This place of history and streets and buildings and names
and people of this place
—named Germantown.

IT IS WITH CONSIDERABLE DIFFICULTY THAT I REMEMBER THE ORIGINAL ERA OF MY BEING

The street with the house where a phone rang wasn't named
for anyone—before it wasn't named for anyone, it was named
for a house named for a person named Loudoun.

Later there will be a history.

Later this comes to be clearer.

Always there will be coming more and more of it.

In the meantime—there was a house—called a premise
or a messuage—on a street named for no one—a street
intersecting with another—a street named after a general
—a madman named Wayne—who had streets and towns
and train stations and people like Batman named after him
—for his deeds.

On the deed to the premise or the messuage it was written—
that the premise or the messuage extended—it extended—
for sixteen feet along Wyneva—and for ninety-seven feet
towards an alley—an alley that extended between streets
named Keyser and Knox—both of whom were men
before they were streets.

Now there is here a beginning.

A beginning of a history from their beginning.

I am certain of this thing.

I've come a long way to come back again to the very
beginning—the beginning that is with us through all
of our living—the beginning that is a place or a site—a site
of linoleum and leaded glass—of remnants and transoms
and babies—a site where a phone rings.

A black box of a phone rings on the wall of a house
of the eighth-born baby—a house not an airlite but a shotgun
or a railroad—someone is calling a number that begins
with a letter to note a beginning—V for an 8, I for a 4,
VI to stand for Victor—a mnemonic to aid in memory.

            I listen and come back again and again to listen.

The phone on the wall rings on the wall with news
of the eighth-born baby—the youngest daughter
of the youngest daughter of the youngest daughter is born
—the one a mother called—the extra one of mine on the line.

            Let's call this my earliest memory.

Let's call this earliest memory of me, my memory.

            I will now begin a description of another one.

Because stories begin everywhere even on streets named
for no one—another way to begin is by saying where we went
and what we held onto—St. Francis and frankincense—
Acme on Ashmead—Lemon Joy and pepper pot—
trolley tracks and trolley straps or Wayne Junction into town.

It was enough for them to hold.

To hold themselves together to them.

Hold as a whole one of this together.

To hold as a whole one when one is thinking of them.

Considering my low beginnings, these were great things to me.

MOVING THROUGH A COUNTRY IS NEVER DONE QUICKLY

It is difficult to begin a story when one is far away from the beginning when there was a little house, a lot of children, not a lot of money and a lot of neighbors.

(Perhaps everything will come to be showing something. And that will be the happy ending of all this beginning.)

Outside the rowhouse not an airlite but a shotgun or a railroad were the neighbors, and some of the neighbors were new and some of the neighbors were old, but most of the neighbors, by the time I came to the house, were new, or so they told me. My siblings told me that before I came to the house new neighbors moved in and old neighbors moved out, and all of this happened very quickly, they said, the moving vans like magic, they said, so quickly they called it flying.

The old neighbors flew like birds from the new neighbors, the neighbors fleeing a fever, a flu that shared its name with a bird. They flew, the old neighbors, to houses next to houses with people who looked like them. But we didn't fly with them. We didn't fly away the way other white people who looked like us did.

And this might have been because of money. I say might because these changes were not discussed or explained, but there were many children and not a lot of money so this reason seems reasonable. Or maybe we didn't fly away the way others who looked like us did because of a feeling. I say maybe because these feelings were not discussed or explained but there was an exchange, my sister told me, much later, my sister told me our mother had asked her a question, a question not meant to be answered, a question about a feeling, the question was, *how would you feel if you moved into a new house and all your new neighbors moved away?* Or maybe we didn't fly away because of the church. I say maybe

36

because these details were not discussed or explained, but much later I heard about a meeting, a meeting at the church where the men of the church, the priests, told the neighbors not to sell their houses, they told the white neighbors not to sell their houses to black people. That to do so would be the beginning of the end.

I need to go back before the beginning. Beginning a new thing without leaving the last thing. Always compelling to understand the reason. All the doing and the moving. Moving through a country is never done quickly. Not like moving vans like magic this place of seeking and pushing and fleeing and living, pushing and living and seeking and fleeing. Projects like this take time.

Much earlier than any of this, Franklin had a project. He wrote, *let all things have their places*. He ruled each page with red ink to keep track of his rights and his wrongs. And I return to him as I return to the surveyors and their maps, the maps made long after Franklin, the maps made before any meetings or moving vans like magic, the maps relating traits of individuals to whole groups of individuals, the maps ruled with lines and shades to grade areas by color.

One map contained a house on a street named for no one. The street was shaded yellow to signify transition, a shade meaning an area at risk of infiltration, of infiltration by what the mapmakers called *a lower grade population*.

From time to time.

Twenty years after this map was drawn, my father bought a house on a street shaded yellow. He bought his house from a woman who looked like him, on a street full of people who looked like him, surrounded by streets full of people who looked like him, and then there was a meeting. It was around this time there was a meeting at the church, the church where my mother and father were married, the church where they baptized their babies, the church where there was a meeting that my parents may or may not have gone to where the priests told the neighbors not to sell their houses. A little later than this, people who looked like my father started buying houses in places far away from the streets on the maps shaded yellow.

It was around this time that there was a burning, a burning at my uncle's house after he sold his house to someone who didn't look like him. Someone who looked like my uncle burned a cross on his lawn, and his baby remembers, my uncle's baby remembers, she tells me about ash on the lawn in the morning. And she tells me so 40 years later.

It was around the time of the burning that all of my father's brothers and all of my mother's sisters drove all of their children to houses next to houses of people who looked like them. Old neighbors moved out and new neighbors moved in, and all of this happened very quickly, they said, but moving through a country is never done quickly, what happens quickly is a story short of details, a story short on details I am telling.

I am telling you that it's likely that if my father had more money or less children or a car or a different religion or a desire to change or a desire to not change or a greater or lesser desire to keep everything exactly the same, we would have flown away the way others who looked like us did, but these things were not discussed or explained and we didn't and I am explaining that.

From time to time on pieces of paper such thoughts.

I sit down to write them for you.

TO FILL UP A PLACE WHEN SOMEONE HAS LOST OUT OF THEM A PIECE

> *The pleasure of a ruin [is] to reconstruct in the*
> *mind's eye the structure in its original state.*
> *The better one [understands] the ruin, the better*
> *the imaginative reconstruction.*
> —M.W. Thompson

The Franklin Exchange was a phone bank,
a bank of princess phones
arranged in a basement
that visitors could dial
for the purpose of retrieving
recordings of famous people
remarking on Benjamin Franklin.

I want to say Gertrude Stein was there
with a Paris exchange that
would take a while to dial,
but her presence is my bad
memory, a transposing
with George Sand whose voice
over the phone told us
Franklin made her cry.

It was always 1976
at the Benjamin Franklin Underground Experience,
and I was a Philadelphian,
lively in the feeling of loving,
standing with my father
who would be dead
in three years,
but I didn't know that then,
it was just 1976.

Let's call this my earliest memory.

The experience was a museum
under a ghost house, a skeleton,
where Franklin's house
had stood before it was razed.
The ghost house, the skeleton
in the shape of a house for which
few records remained,
intended to remind visitors
of the limits of historical knowledge.
They said it was no use
trying to reproduce Franklin's house.
The records were too few, they were
outnumbered by memories.
So let's create a museum instead,
underground and accessible via a ramp,
a red ramp to invoke a colonial road,
which would allow visitors to descend
into the foundation of what had been
Franklin's house. And a hall of mirrors.
Mirrors adorned with neon lights spelling out
Franklin's various selves. Mirrors
and their neon lights designed
to inspire visitors to reflect
on our own various selves.

  IT WAS 1976 IN PHILADELPHIA
  AND WE WERE ALL BENJAMIN FRANKLIN.

The experience would become a time capsule
in museum practice.
Decades later, they said,
the museum did not contribute
to the historical significance of the site,
not in the same way that the ghost house did,
so it would be dismantled
down to its skeleton
upon which a new body
would be built,
under the skeleton
of the house that remains
today, significant
in its inadequacy.

THE ONE READING THE LETTER THEN HAS NOT IN THEM ANY MEMORY OF THE PERSON THAT ONCE WROTE THAT LETTER

And to him I called myself the youngest
and to me he called himself the oldest
and together we played games in the backyard.

Little word games with tiled letters near a rose bush.
Games I don't remember playing but that were mentioned
in a letter. My oldest father, he called himself, in a letter.

How he wrote it down for me.
How much he liked the little word games
we played near a rosebush.

How he felt a little stronger each day,
each day as he was becoming his oldest,
the oldest he would be and still be living.

How there would be little else of his living in me but this:
what he had written down for me in his very last letter.

THEY WILL EXIST EVEN WHEN THEY WON'T, OR,
THIS THEN WILL BE A DESCRIPTION OF THAT THING

Before the street with the house where a phone rang wasn't named for anyone—it was named for a house named for a person named Loudoun—a house where no one lived—a house that means nothing to history—a house in the background of a neighborhood.

And before the house came to mean nothing to history—it was a house full of people who had things like streets named after them—a man named Armat and his daughters Sara and Jane.

In the only history of the house I could find—a paper I found on the internet—the author said Sara was not of sound mind—she spoke in broken sentences—it was difficult for her to form sentences—it was difficult for her to form ideas—she would put a finger in the corner of her eye and utter some ideas she had formed—when she came of age, her father's father who shared her name, and a man named Skerrett—took her money away.

The paper said when Jane came of age, she married her cousin—who shared her name, but who died like her father, so she married Skerrett, a banker who liked to buy furniture—together they bought lots of furniture for their house in the country named Loudoun.

Then Jane and Skerrett had a daughter named Anna who married a man whose father's father's father was a Logan—the Logan who knew so much about books he told Ben Franklin which books to put in his library—and the two of them together—Anna and the Logan—were not very happy. He left her alone with the children and she kept track of his comings and goings—she kept track of the days he left her alone with the children—the days he left her for drink or the maid—then she left him and she kept all her money—she left him and got some of his—somehow she managed this in the time she was living—she managed this—he must have been a monster.

And after the two of them died—two of their children lived in the house and took pictures of all of their things—they took pictures of the parlor and the fireplace and the hemlock—they took pictures of the hickory and their specimen marble table—they took pictures of their paintings, their chairs, and their chandelier—they took pictures of their dog—their dog named Beautiful Witch.

Then the last living one of the family—died—then the last living one named Maria—gave the house away to the city—she gave the house to the city where it sat—where it sat with its things and its pictures of things—the galloons and the fringe—the socks and the sheets and the shoes.

After Maria died there was a war—and a distant relation—a Logan—who liked the histories of things—used the house to collect things for the war—this distant relation liked her family's place in history—she liked things—and she and the ladies she invited to the house collected things in the house for the war—then the war ended—and the house and its things went back to their sitting—so a caretaker sat with its lamps and the linens, the plates and the harp, the diaries, the paintings, and the fabrics.

Then a woman arrived—a woman in pearls—a woman looking for a cause, who redecorated—she liked the people who used all the things, she liked Anna so much she took her diary—she took the diary where Anna described her husband and what he did to her— she took the diary that Anna wrote in in French like a code—she took the diary and hid it and no one knows where it is.

This woman this friend—invited people to the house—but people rarely came—the people nearby didn't care for the house or its things—the people far away didn't care for the people nearby—so people didn't come and the house sat with its things—with its harp in the window and its galloons and the fringe in the attic.

It was around this time that I came to know the house, not its peo-
ple—the house with its grounds that became a park—where my
sister looked for her things after some of her things were stolen by
thieves—and like her things, the house became increasingly vul-
nerable—its caretakers wrote about break-ins—about people tear-
ing up bricks from its lovely brick walk—about ripping up bricks
and throwing them—the caretakers wanted protection from van-
dals, the thieves, the neighbors—they wanted money for pendants
they could wear around their necks—they wanted pendants that
would transmit their panic—they wrote letters describing it—about
a situation you couldn't understand unless you were experiencing
it yourself.

Then later the house was struck by lightning—the lightning caused
a fire—many things are believed to have been destroyed in the
fire—many things remain in places unknown—but some things
were archived or so they tell me—someone told me about a list of
all the things that had been saved.

The list said:

some of the things that remain are portraits
of the family   a portrait of Anna   a sampler

and a folding needle case

a needle case a friendship needle pincushion   plates

a saucer with a figure holding a sword

three cans and a saucer   a sauce boat

a small tea cup with a saucer   a saucer a soup plate

soup plate soup plate cup and saucer saucer two plates
and a bowl   two cups and a saucer

a bowl with flower swags a plate broken in half and repaired

        soup bowl soup bowl soup bowl soup bowl

     a soup bowl broken in two pieces   a charger
        a charger

        a shell-shaped dish   a round scalloped-edge
bowl

        a round scalloped-edge bowl a deep scalloped
bowl

          an oval dish with scalloped edge

        sauce tureen sauce tureen and matching ladle
saucer for a sauce tureen   saucer for a sauce tureen

        footed bowl or compote

            dog figurine a cream pitcher

     charger charger charger silhouette   pistol

        a box of assorted marble samples

     one specimen marble table

and a Grecian wine cup
     a skyphos
        from the second half of the 4th century
              BCE.

IT IS HARD FOR AN EMPTY SACK TO STAND Ben

On the corner of Wayne once a man
and Wyneva once Loudoun—was a lot once a building
—a grassy lot in place of a brick building with brick porches
on a brick road for firm footing—the building
was named for a street named for no one—a name
given without regard to the old world—the Wyneva.

Before the building was a lot it was a vacant—
a place to buy drugs or to squat—before it was a squat
it was section 8 housing or an SRO—and before it was an SRO
it was a hotel or apartments or a place where couples
like my parents could hold wedding receptions.

—And none of that was recorded on the internet.

To search.

Sometimes what we come to know is what is lost
after others don't care to know it—this lot once a squat
is coming to mean something about what records get recorded.

To make that recollection as durable as possible
by putting it down
in writing.

Someone who lives across the street from the lot once a squat—
doesn't want to talk to me about it—she's happy it's gone—
she's safer it's gone—Allison—she wants to talk to me
about the playground across the street
—the hollow once a quarry—maybe the city's
first playground—Happy Hollow—
she wants a garden not guns in the hollow once a quarry
but everything's a struggle.

Maybe she heard the shots that killed Vincent Parsons
when police chased him through the hollow on Good Friday
                    —such force such fire—
        someone said—
        they weren't supposed to open fire in a playground—
                                someone said
            —we cleared the area of children first.

The lot once a squat leaves behind few records
—but Allison tells me where I can find a picture of it.

                    Get the picture to exist.

                    To make real this thing.

                    In pieces to me.

A file folder on the fifth floor of City Hall contains a record
                    —pieces of perhaps a whole one—it says—
the repeated cutting up of a building shows a history
of a neighborhood's inability to create housing
for people who don't own homes.

                    To be in pieces in repeating the whole one.

The record says—that after years of no heat
and open fires—the building was unfit for habitation—it says—
its frail and elderly tenants—including the building owner's
mother—refused to leave.

                    Building it up by little pieces.

The record says—the building lacked distinction
                    —that the Wyneva is no Alden Park—
the pink building like a castle, like a cake, off the Wissahickon—
where my parents had their wedding reception.

Always they are in pieces then.

Pieces of a record on a table.

To make real this thing.

A ruin of hedges and vestibules.

That moldy pissy brick smell.

This lot once a squat is coming to mean something
about what records are kept in the body—like the body
of a builder—the son of a bricklayer—a builder
of brick buildings who built the Wyneva in 1911—a builder
who went missing in 1915—he went missing
in a gray suit and straw hat—the police searched and searched
for the smooth-shaven builder—who suffered from overwork—
who suffered from a nervous condition—they searched
until they found his body in a creek—not far
from another brick building—another brick building
he had built.

LET ALL YOUR THINGS HAVE THEIR PLACES

> *It would be misleading to think that preservation is successful only when buildings are saved from destruction. Collective memory in modern capitalist culture is a process—a continual ebb and flow of remembering and forgetting—and only one among many processes shaping the built environment as citizens experience it.*
> —Randall Mason

A mindful collection, this collection of things. To build a site that orders and secures. To order and secure an avenue, a factory, a station. To preserve a site is to provide permanence, a hook upon which to fasten memory. What is salvaged, preserved: the material links to the past, the artifacts. What to guard against: the rendering of artifacts apart from the living, the living who give a site meaning. Meaning the skin that holds us together. Making a place for us together as living.

THE ANXIETIES WHICH THE STATE OF WAR OCCASIONED

*Preserving the memory of its wild and romantic
incidents in some tangible form, and of saving its
history from that oblivion of the grave, which will soon
envelope the survivors of the Revolution.*
—George Lippard

First,
a certain quaintness:
roofs along a great road.

What a storyteller called,
an Indian file of houses.

A story that is repeated in the history of this place.
A story that means something to history so I tell it.
A history of all the endings
that make up so many of our beginnings—

War.

How it was then—
all night and fear
before battle day.

There,
on the great road.

The people having
but one feeling in them:
the terror of living
in an occupied city.

To anticipate shrieking.
A feeling in the body.
Holding onto that feeling
                    and its hold.

Fog.

A shot through the mist
and a war shout from Wayne—
a madman who would have streets and towns
and people like Batman named after him.
General Mad Anthony Wayne
at Washington's side.
Men who'll become streets
intersecting.

A war shout from Wayne,
the warrior-drover,
and the soldiers advance
upon a mansion—the Chew house
and its occupiers.

They advance.
Blood down the walls,
wine down the walls,
barrels in the attic in the belly shot open.
The soldiers, they drink, the debauch of death,
the ludicrous horror, the blood goblets.
Battle smoke renders all senses, all objects dim.
                    All hurry and tramp and motion.

They fight until they fall.
A common ending.

But in this retelling
—the retelling I'm rewriting—
the last shot is taken by a rebel:
a man of strange and wild aspect
of scarred face unshaven
who jumps over a wall of a graveyard,
who jumps over a wall to kill an occupier,
Agnew, an occupier who had a premonition
that he would die that day
because he walked out the death door
at Grumblethorpe.

Grumblethorpe, another house on a great road
somewhere between a mansion and a graveyard.
A house named for a house in a story,
a story named *Thinks I to Myself.*

      There,
in a house
of imagination and music
is a beginning.

Grumblethorpe,
the site of America's first gingko tree,
where a gardener tells me:

      life tumbles all over itself here.

A GOOD PAPER WOULD SCARCELY FAIL

Very little is known about the mill
and its beginnings.
Some of what is known
comes from a poem.

The first poem
printed on paper from the mill.

from Linnin Rags good Paper doth derive

The first poem
printed in the middle colonies.

the first trade keeps the second Trade alive

A poem that is retold
as I move through a little house
with another little house inside it.
Another little house with figures inside it
who move about to tell the story of a mill.

Pieces of perhaps a whole one.

a creek to turn a mill
a wheel to turn a stamp
a stamp hammering rags into stuff

a vatman to scoop stuff with a shake
a coucher couching paper between felt
a rhythm to press and then rest

flax rags to pulp and then paper

A whole one in pieces makes another.

Very little is known about the mill
and what brought about its ending.
Some of what is known
comes from wasps,
from watching wasps
spin paper from trees,
a method of milling the mill couldn't do,
so it ended.

This is what I've come to know about a mill near a creek.

        The creek   an agitated swan

   a wrinkle:
             the Wissahickon.

      Named for its catfish or color.

             A Lenni-Lenape name.

   A creek near a drive
          named forbidden.

      A drive not meant for drivers
      but feet.

            Here,

  in the Wissahickon

         a path through schist

         a book unstitched

     pages of a creek and what's remembered.

What is remembered in what is written down about them:

A bench for Brian who lived to picnic.

A bench for Mitchell my present husband.

A bench for Buzz on the 10th anniversary of his 40th birthday.

A bench that tells me every thing changes always.

A bench that tells me to live the life I have imagined.

A bench where I stop somewhere
waiting for you.
Here I wait and here you are:

A heron.

To catch one's breath.

To hold on to the life of it—

by putting it down in writing.

HAVING BEEN BUILT TO BE FUNCTIONAL

The very concept of a historic district suggests that
the district as a whole constitutes the principal
historic resource and possesses greater
significance than its individual component parts.
—Philadelphia Historical Commission

A history of all the feeling—the history of this one—
where more trains stopped than anywhere in the world—
where my father noticed my mother for the first time—where
three men beat another man till he died—where conductors
assumed they already took my ticket—where they assumed
I hadn't gotten on.

The station—a place—named for a general and a man—
who had streets and towns and people like Batman
named after him—a junction named Wayne and the surrounding
buildings—are now a district—designated historic—to preserve
an industrial heritage.

A skin to hold them in.

To hold as a whole one when one thinks about them.

Mill buildings around a station—signs etched in stone—
ball-bearings, pencils, pushpins, silk—signs of things made—
to make a living.

One who looks at them gets the history.

To make a living from little pins.

Where pushpins were made before any other pushpins were
made—well set in the glass, the steel pin would not bend—
a pushpin factory now a rehab.

To make a living.

Where paper pencils were made before any other paper pencils
were made—unravel the paper to draw out the point—
skin-marking pencils to mark the wounded in war—glass-marking
pencils to make marks that remain
—now it's a vacant, waiting to be razed.

This one was a whole one.

This one held together by a skin.

Mill buildings around a station—one holds a church—another
a tree—

The one who wants a garden not guns
in the hollow once a quarry says people find out about things
by seeing them—but some people don't see things till they're
gone.

One building remains in use as a mill—a mill that makes
tapes and braids—cords and trims—spools and dyes—

The pieces that hold the parts together.

SOME WOMEN HAVE ALL THEIR LIVING THEIR SCHOOL FEELING

A school with a long history has at least one story
that gets repeated.

That story is this—

A teacher took a student's iPod away, and the student pushed
the teacher into a hallway—he pushed the teacher
into another student in the hallway—into another student
who just reacted—who just reacted by punching the teacher
—by punching the teacher in the head with a lock.

The teacher remembers nothing about the punching—he lost
some of his memory—he lost some of his ability to remember
things—the way he can't remember his story
is part of his story—sometimes when he tells his story
he forgets which parts he wants to tell.

*

Sometimes people use his story to tell stories they want to tell
about memory and history and schools.

Like the story of how the school came to be—
how the school came to be because of trolleys and bodies.

That story is this—

Over a hundred years ago—the men of the neighborhood,
the men in the mansions, said they needed a neighborhood
high school—a high school to protect their daughters—to protect
their daughters from the strange men and crazy dance halls—
from the strange men and crazy dance halls their daughters
had to pass by when they rode the trolley to the only school
that would have them—a school far away they had to get to

by trolley—and the men of the city listened to the men
in the mansions and they built the men's daughters a school.

It was a story about trolleys and bodies and girls—
the bodies where girls learn all of their living.
Sometimes people use this story
to tell stories they want to tell
about trolleys and bodies and living.
                    That story is this—

Much later there was another school at the end of a trolley line,
a school named for a saint who liked to hide—
who liked to be little—
who wished to be perfect by becoming still less—
a saint with the name little flower—it was a school
where a mother had gone and her sisters had gone
and her daughters had gone to
by trolley.

The school I would have gone to—had there not been a body
in my way.

                    This is a story I haven't told before.

The way I haven't told this story is part of my story—sometimes

            when I start to tell this story—

                    I stop.

                    The story is this—

—there was a body in my way.

For years the body of a white man with white hair was always
watching, was always waiting—in an alley in a window

in a doorframe on a porch in the summer in the winter he'd be
                    naked—his body
                    more often than not
          was not clothed but naked—a monster in a sight line
—a neighbor.

The white man with white hair had a bicycle
he could ride with no hands—with no hands up a hill he was
strong—
a bicycle he would ride with a hole in his pants—
a hole he had cut in the back of his pants—a hole
he would show me by standing.

And one day from his bicycle he told me he loved me—and I
ran away to tell someone, and she said, are you sure?
                    —and when she said, are you sure?
nothing changed—nothing changed but
          bodies—
                    bodies that hide.

          All the unprotected surface of them.

A body afraid to leave a house by the front door
because of a monster in a sight line learns to hide
—learns to go out the back door and hold one's breath—
(that moldy pissy brick smell)—this can go on for years
                    —back and forth out the back door
                                        a way of living—

          Keeping out of danger was all there was of living.
          Sometimes repeating is all that there is of them.

                                        *

This is the story of how schooling came to be in me—a body
afraid to leave a house by a front door will take a bus

out the back to a different school altogether—a different school named for a city not a saint—a school named for a city and its girls—a school with the motto, she conquers who conquers herself.

This is the story of how schooling came to be in me—and like some stories it went on for a long time till it stopped—till it just stopped, suddenly, like this—

One day I left the house to pick up a new pair of eyeglasses
—to be able to see again clearly—
and on that same day, he picked up and left—
away from the porch and the alley and his house.
I couldn't believe it—I watched—from inside the house
from a threshold of a bedroom—from far away
from the window—I watched—I watched for days, for weeks,
or longer—I watched till I could be sure
he was gone.

Looking so as to be sure.

To build up certainty with little and little sure things.

This is a story about what records are kept in the body.

The bodies where we learn all of our living.

A USEFUL PIECE GAVE RISE TO A PROJECT

> *Color is the glass. Shadow is the paint.*
> —Bryan Willette, glass artist

Across the street from the hollow once a quarry
sits a garage full of color and shards.
A garage full of glass and its makers.
The makers and all their little pieces.

They showed me how to make a whole one from traces.

How to choose the right piece of glass for color,
        to lay the pieces of glass out on a table,
                to keep going until the glass matches a pattern,
to add shadow to a scene by scratching,
        to fuse all the colors with a flame,
                to pound the glass into a heart and solder.

They showed me how to make a beginning from an ending.

Like the church around the corner that had closed,
        the church where my mother and father were married,
                the church where they baptized their babies,
the church whose ending was the beginning of this writing,
                whose windows the makers took to make again.

The makers and all their beginnings.

We are tearing all the saints from their places.
Releasing colors from their ribbons of lead.

THE SENSE OF BEGINNING OR OF ENDING

How do I begin to write about the church whose ending was the beginning of this writing?

St. Francis

    brittle pamphlet

Inside a parish history published for its 50th anniversary in 1949, my grandfather's name appears on the inside cover, written in what looks like my mother's hand.

    a jubilee year

from the Latin

      to shout for joy

A man named Francis I never met.

A book I took years ago from my mother's credenza, from the Italian for belief.

Its pages flake as I turn them.

It took a lot of fundraising to
raise the church. Wage-earning
families were urged to fund a
lasting memorial for their
children's children, for the
thousands yet unborn.

to take shape

    in a place

of creeks   rocks   and weeds

          here
in obedience   they said

          here   to be pure
and honest

     here   to give your life
to this work
       in an age that needs
       your example

In Assisi, Francis spent money
with lavish hand until he met the
lepers and built his house of reeds.
Clare joined him in his mission.

They called her a princess of poverty. My mother's confirmation name was Clare.

to confirm   an initiation

it roots us more deeply

the name a protector and guide

After building a church, they built a school. The pastor said he could always identify a Catholic-schooled woman through the nobility and humility of her bearing, through her desire to imitate the violet—unseen, unheard, known only by its fragrance.

to begin then with a nose

to perceive a smell

or else pry, search.

I remember a homeless woman with a ring of empty seats around her.

wish her peace and get a stink on you

There—
in the church where my mother and father were married
the church where they baptized their babies
where his coffin, but not hers, would be incensed

a thurible swings

a mist to lift prayer
to see
a kind of faith
to follow

Another way to begin then is to
say what I saw. What I saw when
I returned. When I returned to the
church after many years away. To
see it on the day that it was ending.

Windows.

The work of an Irishman
who drew the faces of his ancestors into the glass

all their long faces and fingers and toes

Names.
A bulletin board for those who served in the war

each letter a pin

asterisk marks a death

A war that gave work to those fleeing a fever, that flu

in the South that drove people here,
to this place where the people they'd work for
would fly away.

Birds.

eagle for a lectern

peacock for a painting

a Jesus all wing and red flame

The man who said: before the war, no one ever left here,
but after seeing the world in war, we wanted to see more
of the world, so we moved away.

The girl who said: my father was taken from me, he's in
prison, so this church has been really important to me.

the weight
of so much unsaid

To begin then with an incomplete recounting.

Another way to begin is to keep going.

It's two years after the church's
closing and I'm in the archives.
It's the day before my mother's
birthday, the first one since her
passing.

she   who repeated

you don't have to like
                    everyone but you do
            have to love them

a sentiment of kindness,
or dilemma

                              In a box of ephemera, I find a
                              photo album from the church's
                              100th anniversary labeled "A
                              Welcome Back Mass."

            the women my mother drank coffee with

    the men who went off to war

                              At the very end there's a picture
                              of the church on an empty corner.
                              The way a corner looks after
                              people have left it. No, that's not
                              right. The way it looks when
                              those who remain are inside.
                              Like my mother. Who didn't
                              need to be welcomed back, who
                              remained. For years. With the
                              neighbors whose practice was
                              living and a faith grown strong in
                              repeating.

completely living her everyday living

for her husband whose heart broke from working

and her children who left handprints down the wall

> It's two years after the church's closing, and I'm in the archives. I find a yearbook from 1934, my father's junior class, and a description of a school play, in which one student played "a darkie boy with remarkable facility."

beyond this dusty room

in the streets of a new century

people are chanting,

Don't shoot.

> It's two years after the church's closing, and I'm in the archives. I find annual reports tracking the numbers of people in the parish. How many were baptized or married or died. How many people in 1957 are "colored." And how many are "Negro." For years. For years, they asked how many, how many, until 1983 when they ask how many of the

people are "Black." Annual reports that ask in 1967 have you talked to your people about fair housing, have you talked to your people about racial justice. Questions they ask the next year and then stop.

to document:
another form of beginning

It's two years after the church's closing, and I'm in the archives. I find pamphlets from the '60s full of advice for parents. A warning against the use of racial epithets. It says don't turn slurs into the air your children breathe.

months later   or decades

people are screaming,

We can't breathe.

In this room full of dust I can taste it: the gleanings and failures of an archive, and those of the people I come from, who I'm coming to know, through all they held on to and all they let go.

After the church closed, the man who learned to make stained glass from the son of the man who made the windows in the church removed them from the church piece by piece. Only then did he notice that a saint's legs were upside down.

pelvis for ankle

red sash interrupted

He said:
It can be difficult for a maker to see the whole when focusing on its pieces.

fragile scrapbook

a cigar box full of medals

He said:
It can be difficult for a maker to admit mistakes after completing the whole.

I look down to touch them:

the rust on my shirt

the dirt under all of my nails

A PREVAILING RED

And the place was brick.

Corner
      porch
            road
cold radiator row,
            my life

in a city of brick.
      My mother and I
          born
          in lines
          of mud and fire and red.

      My father,
          along
          train tracks
             after time clocks,
    clocked her legs

at the station.
      A seam to follow.
    He bore the weight
of lead type
and failed strikes

to tend a line
of babies that filled
their rowhouse of brick.
He saw his wife
       fall to pieces

washing dishes.
     She, who worried
         stains
         on plates
         till she broke.

I mourn her,
      ill at ease
      in the kitchen, always
working, a steady working,
long after her children

were fed and in bed,
tucked in
like sardines.
      Did she giggle
         as a girl?

      He helped her mind
         the children, carry
food from the store,
the canned fruit, the soup.
         They'd make use

of every scrap.
A splash of milk
on rice to make a pudding.
With little, they
kept us full.

He tried to mend
her head
and hold our hands.
To keep it all together,
he worked.

His hands cast
lines of type—
magazine characters
of molten lead.
He knew printing.

While one line
was cast
he'd start the next.
To keep up
with the work

till it ran out.
To be counted on.
A new
means, a new dead means
of production.

He could not,
like a slug,
bend once cool.
      Again and again he was struck
         by layoffs.

As to their bright new
         baby, the last in line,
   so late, his eighth:
      a heart
      can't haul

such weight
in middle age.
     All the walking,
     the waking. A long
         line of babies.

Too heavy
to pick up.
His shiny penny.
     So many pennies
     in his thoughts.

    I grew
in crowded rooms,
and concrete,
skated on lakes
of brick and scabbed.

Grew
reading
on radiators—
flesh pressed
into iron.

Grew
on routes,
the trains,
the lines
inscribed in memory.

And now I, a stray,
      keyboard for claw
            without pause
                 wander
      my history

of brick—
    To bring forth
    a city:
              sing
its repeating.

    Markers.
A moment of stillness
at seven.
And so young.
Seven years, one death.

One dress:
a dusky mauve rose
      saved for those
      events that mark
             a life, a rite.

      A line of people greeting
      a line of people
      grieving. The man
            who whispered, I never
saw him angry, in my ear.

Solemnities.
What kind of stone
      to place
on his grave
unless

      a pillow.
To rest.
A straphanger
      in life. In death
      he lay

in wait of her
to join him
in bed again.
      How much less am I
      in the dark than they?

Ritual held sway in them.
    Scripture
        like brick
grows strong
    in repeating.

And in those
    who splinter—schist—
        in us exists
        an impulse to disrupt
the things we thought we knew—

    like a city:
    full of histories
    that shift.
        I go away
and come back again

never really knowing the streets
named for no one
and madmen.
        Who were they—
    she,

who made the beds,
    he, who rode the train,
    they, who left
        handprints
           down the wall,

I, with block rattle
in my bones, aware
that at any moment
a light can burn out
or be shot.

O this constructed life.
Do not lose time
lost in memory
so easily
ruined

by inattention or intention.
Build it up again
in little pieces—
all that we carry
or are coming to know.

True, I possess
a sense
of threat—
cats, mouths heavy
with birds, at the door—

memory, that body
where we learn all of our living.
But, now, this body
far from hardship,
recalls, also, lightning

bugs in the yard, and knows
it was not always
                              torturous
            under
the street light.

                    Here I am, after all.
              I walk and write
and scratch my name
                    into histories
                    of brick.

Germantown Courier

25¢

The Oldest Weekly Newspaper in Pennsylvania

GERMANTOWN PA., WEDNESDAY FEBRUARY 24, 1982

46—NO. 15

Wyneva Tenants Elude City's Help

How Many Actually Live There Is Unknown

By Rick Linsk
Courier Staff Writer

The city Welfare Department is trying to relocate tenants of the Wyneva Hotel, but faced with the refusal of some to leave, hopes for a court order to shut the building.

The Wyneva, 4901 Wayne Avenue, was declared unfit for habitation last month, but a small number of residents will not cooperate with the Welfare Department's Relocation Services staff.

"This has been happening every winter," said Louis Souder of the

said to live there. There is also a group of squatters now in several units.

The relocation official told of one man who was taken from the Wyneva recently and placed in a nearby boarding home. The man left the home shortly after arriving there, and though Souder is not sure, he thinks the man went back to the hotel. He also believes other tenants went back.

"The boarding home operator told me the guy left and he didn't know where he went," he said.

If the tenants refuse to leave or insist on returning to the Wyneva, then a court order

Philadelphia Historical Commission
Research Request Form
(Form must be filled out in ink and it must be legible)

Name (Please Print): SUE LANDERS

Occupation:

Organization/Affiliation:

Files and/or material requested: 4901 WAYNE AVE
4821 Greene St   4650 Germantown Ave

Purpose of research: POETRY

Signature: _____   Date: 9/5/12

Wayne Junction National Historic District: Wayne Avenue and Berkley Street, taken from the roof of the Max Levy building (top); inside Wayne Mills, the district's remaining operating factory (bottom).

Franklin Court, Old City, Philadelphia: Architects Venturi, Scott Brown, and Associates' "ghost structure," where Franklin's house once stood (top); the phone bank in the original Benjamin Franklin Underground Museum (bottom).

The Winston Building in Center City, Philadelphia (left) where my
father worked for 25 years before the union was busted, now luxury lofts.
The letter my father wrote me two days before he died (right).

My mother and father, with her parents, at their wedding reception outside
Alden Park near Wissahickon and Chelten Avenues, 1954 (top). Alden Park,
2012 (bottom).

Remaining structures at Rittenhousetown, the first paper mill in the United States (top). A "half-house" on Wayne Avenue near Queen Lane (bottom).

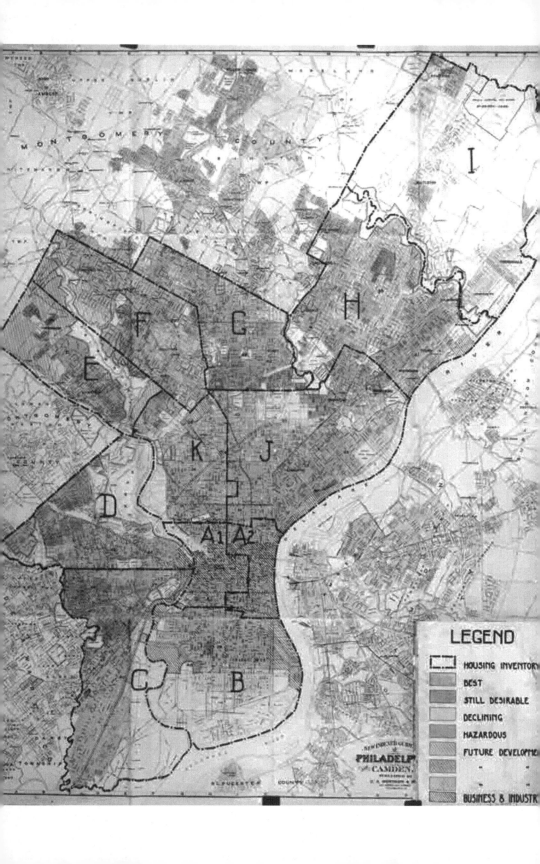

LEGEND

HOUSING INVENTORY
BEST
STILL DESIRABLE
DECLINING
HAZARDOUS
FUTURE DEVELOPME
" "
" "
BUSINESS & INDUSTR

St. Anthony of Padua
St. Joseph
Ambler

LOCATIONS OF OTHER CHURCHES, LISTED BY NUMBER

1. ST. ADALBERT (Polish) — E. Allegheny Ave. & Thompson St.
2. ST. AGNES (Slovak) — 4th and Brown Sts.
3. ST. ALOYSIUS (German) — 26 th and Tasker Sts.
4. ST. ALPHONSUS (German) — 4600 South 4 th St.
5. ST. ANDREW (Lithuanian) — 19 th and Wallace Sts.
6. ST. ANDREW'S CHAPEL (Lithuanian) — 1123 Lemon St.
7. ST. BONAVENTURE (German) — 9th and Cambria Sts.
8. ST. BONIFACE (German) — Diamond and Hancock Sts.
9. ST. CASIMIR (Lithuanian) — 326 - 28 Wharton St.
10. ST. CATHERINE of SIENNA (Colored) — 626 West Pine St.
11. ST. DONATO (Italian) — 65 th and Callowhill Sts.
12. ST. GEORGE (Lithuanian) — 3700 E. Venango St.
13. ST. HEDWIG (Polish) — 311 North 23rd St.
14. ST. HENRY (German) — 4400 North 5 th St.
15. HOLY REDEEMER CHAPEL (Chinese) — 915 Vine St.
16. HOLY TRINITY (German) — 6 th And Spruce Sts.
17. ST. IGNATIUS of LOYOLA (Colored) — 43rd and Wallace
18. ST. JOHN CANTIUS (Polish) — Thompson and Gallagher Sts.
19. ST. JOHN NEPOMUCEN (Slovak) — 9th and Wharton Sts.
20. ST. JOSAPHAT (Polish) — 142 Cotton St.
21. KING OF PEACE (Italian) — 26 th and Wharton
22. ST. LADISLAUS (Polish) — 16-48 West Hunting Park Ave.
23. ST. LAURENTIUS (Polish) — Memphis and Earl Berks Sts.
24. ST. LUCY (Italian) — 147-55 Green Lane
25. ST. LUDWIG (German) — 28 th and Master Sts.
26. ST. MARK (Armenian) — 6014 Market St.

27. ST. MARON (Maronite Rite) — 10 th and Ellsworth Sts.
28. BLESSED MARTIN DE PORRES (Colored) — 1328 South 22nd St.
29. ST. MARY OF THE ASSUMPTION (Ger.) — 170 Conarroe St.
30. ST. MARY OF CZENSTOCHOWA (Pol.) — 5916 and Ellsworth St.
31. ST. MARY OF THE ETERNAL (Italian) — 23 nd and Clearfield Sts.
32. ST. MARY MAGDALEN DE PAZZI (Ital.) — 714 Montrose St.
33. MATER DOLOROSA (Italian) — Paul and Lippincott Sts.
34. ST. MICHAEL OF THE SAINTS (Ital.) — 4821 German St.
35. ST. MICHAEL'S MISSION (Polish) — Red Lion Road & Papal Junction
36. MOTHER OF DIVINE GRACE (Ital.) — E. Thompson and Camboro Sts.
37. ST. NICHOLAS OF TOLENTINO (Ital.) — 9th and Watkins Sts.
38. OUR LADY OF ANGELS — 50 th and Master Sts.
39. OUR LADY OF THE BLESSED SACRAMENT (Colored) — 712 North Broad St.
40. OUR LADY OF CONSOLATION (Italian) — Princeton and Edmund Sts.
41. OUR LADY HELP OF CHRISTIANS (Ger.) — E. Allegheny Ave and Coal Sts.
42. OUR LADY OF LORETO (Italian) — 6304 Greys Ave.
43. OUR LADY OF THE MIRACULOUS MEDAL — 7003 Spring Garden St. (Sotouth)
44. OUR LADY OF POMPEII (Italian) — 6th and Fitler Ave.
45. ST. PETER THE APOSTLE (German) — 5th and Girard Ave.
46. ST. PETER CLAVER (Colored) — 12th and Lombard Sts.
47. ST. ROCH MISSION (Italian) — Oxford and Anchor Sts.
48. SACRED HEART (Hungarian) — Melcher and Master Sts.
49. ST. STANISLAUS (Polish) — 240 Fitzwater St.
50. ST. JOHN BAPTIST VIANNEY — 36 Jefferson St. West Manayunk
51. ST. LUCY IN MONTE — Jefferson & Price Sts. W. Manayunk

Portraits of Germantown residents: Rocio Cabello and Renny Molenaar, with their sons Giza and Cory (top left), Tieshka Smith (bottom left), Allison Weiss (top right), and sisters Aine and Emaleigh Doley (bottom right).

PART TWO: CONVERSATIONS
this is now a writing of the history as it comes out of some of them

THIS WAS THEN THE WAY I WAS FILLED FULL OF IT AFTER LOOKING

This is a poem about a book about a neighborhood that is a poem—
a poem about a red brick road along a row of little houses—a few
of them lived in and all the people who gather nearby—the acrobat—
the singer—the guy who came out as an astrologer—the sky that
is high and low around them as they gather into that which makes
them—a poem about catfish and waffles—a rib crib with books
pulled out of dragons—rooms cracked open like a time capsule—
happy Secretary Day balloons from 1998 floating half full.

This is a poem about myths full of stuff—a clock like a sun—a
drum struck from a stump—toddlers falling out of screen doors
and a Louis Vuitton trunk that missed the Titanic—a poem bound
by a rose garden with rows wide enough for two—for two to turn
their heads from side to side to smell the roses—a hedge to fence
the joy in.

This is a poem about pulping bibles to make bullets for a revolution—
a bladder full of pokeberry juice—a portrait drawn in blood—
about how impossible it was to get the right kind of mortgage—and
how savage the lenders were in foreclosing—a postcard of a cemetery
with the words still living scrawled across the front.

This is a poem about Sydney telling me we can get there wherever
there is to have a decent life where the poetry happens—a poem
about John and his bowl full of prayers—and Vashti who gets
asked why she doesn't live in Mt. Airy—and Rachael who says
places like this are hard to navigate, all tied up with romance and
symbolism and baggage—a poem about a poem about Kevon who
gave me a hug—and Bernard who gave me a ride—and that guy
who wanted to give me one of his minutes since I didn't have
one—and Tiptoe who called me a vampire.

These are the makings of an autobiography of America. → refering to initial project

THE WATER IN A NATURAL KIND OF WAY IS ALWAYS FLOWING

I asked Adam what he knew about a red brick street.
A red brick street repaved with concrete.
Adam, my sewer enthusiast.
He told me there's no story, just work.
Just work on pipes under a red brick street.
So many bricks to put back that they didn't.
So we took a walk and we talked about streets.
We talked about what runs underneath.
We took a walk and talked about our mothers.
Mine with dementia, his with memories through hospice.
We took a walk to look at maps the size of tables.
Maps we had to walk around to read.
To understand all their meets and their bounds.
Their markers in the shape of maples.
To find your place on a map with a tree.
To see where you are and how much is left till you get there.
The maps that take us back before the beginning.
Before the red brick street was repaved.
Before the street was a street made of brick.
Before the street was a street named for no one.
When the street named for no one was just a creek.
A creek without a name—he took me back.
To show me how water becomes a corner—how water becomes
a hill—how the shape of one thing becomes another—
to become these things we know of as streets.

I LIKE TO LISTEN TO ANYONE I LIKE TO HEAR
THE LIVING THEY HAVE IN THEM

A poem about Virginia who's 91 and has lived
here all her life—mostly in the house she was born in—
a house on a Belgian block road
—Virginia who talks to me a stranger.

        just ordinary enough talking

           to talk about little things

Virginia who always had a man in her life—like the man
who used to live in the home with her—not the house
she was born in but the home where she lives now
with the others—the man who left the home
to live in another—a home he can leave when he wants
to—to have a drink.

Or the son who was born with his eyes wide open—
and who died in the house she was born in—her son who
gave her away at her wedding—her wedding to her first
and only husband—her wedding to the man who adored
her and not the man she doesn't mention
when she mentions her son.

          an ordinary enough telling

this telling and this not telling of things

        the kind of things anyone may find

      themselves telling or not telling

          when talking about living

A poem about Virginia completely living her everyday
living—who has lived here all of her life—and Lorraine
who takes me to meet her—meeting Virginia then
taking a walk with Lorraine—her neighbor.

                        walking around something and
walking around that same thing again

             a church on the corner without windows

       a house on a Belgian block road

                        simply walking
        and then stopping to talk

To talk in a backyard full of living
                —the basil, the groundhog, the figs—
the trampoline, the bathtub, the mulberry.

Simply walking and then stopping to talk—
            a poem about Lorraine weeding wild trees
       while her husband Gerry paints upstairs
—creating beauty in the conditions of living.

I WISHED, IF POSSIBLE, TO IMITATE IT

A poem about Ray who told me:

I'm a dirtball who married a princess—my wife wanted to live in a foreign country so we moved to Texas—when I first got to Texas I never talked about where I came from—when I got here I said, that's all behind me—I didn't leave because of white flight—I really liked Germantown—now I use Google street view and wander all over—when people tell me they hate the way it changed, I ask them so why did you leave.

When I was in fifth grade this nun came into our class and closed the door—she said I have two colored students outside who are going to go to school here—she said they aren't like us but you need to be nice to them—my scoutmaster sold his house to the first black family on the block—then For Sale signs went up all over—that family kept to themselves—I don't remember their names.

My mother had two generations of kids—one before the war and one after—I was a victory baby—my father stoked the furnace at Midvale—he gave my mother $20 a week—she thought boiled celery was a vegetable—my father knew everybody and everybody knew Whitey—I was terrified of him—he beat me for doing things I couldn't do—he sold his house after a lady on the block was murdered—they said she was decapitated—I don't know if that was true—on his deathbed I told him I loved him—he said, you don't have to tell me that—I thought, you miserable old bastard.

I meet people in Texas who do everything they can to seem like they're from here—I may live here, but I'm from Germantown—and that's never going to change—I don't want to be an imitation—I'm living with the history that I have.

HERE ON MY SCRAPS OF PAPER FOR YOU

The internet told me very little about the house except that a man named Mark wrote a paper about it. Mark and I might be the only people interested in the house. We might be the only people on the internet interested in the house. The internet told me very little about the house except that a library had some boxes and the people at the library didn't know what was in them. The people in the library pointed me to a man who had been through the box and that turned out to be Mark, who told me:

> even after the fire destroyed
>
>   so much

a staggering amount
>   of documentation remains   so
>   much   of the ephemera
>   that documents the house and its generations

>   remains

there are those   who want to disperse the collection
>   to sell
>   what they consider unimportant

in most cases   the unimportant
        becomes less so   in context

the image of her dog   Beautiful Witch   as a photograph,
      it could be any image
          but in context   there's a woman
              trying to fill a great void

      to engage herself in pursuits

   pursuits that bury memories of a
      terrible time

          her maniacal pursuits
          her desire to get it right
it survives
      in what survives

I find it all too much.
        Though I can't let it go.

   the curse of the researcher once immersed

       the only way   to get it right
is to read every scrap

     to sift through
          intimacy
    a gold mine

WE LIKED TO KEEP THEM TOGETHER

> *I haven't any little small imperishable objects belonging
> to Whitman. Horace did not inherit any such material.
> There were some pens, which he gave away...He did not
> have any sympathy for souvenirs of that kind. The work!
> The work! interested Horace...But I'll tell you what I
> have got. His nutmeg grater. And I have used it for a
> number of years. Many a glass of sangaree has been
> made...He made sangaree for himself—for his house-
> hold—for sick neighbors—and once or twice for me.*
> —Anne Traubel, former Germantown resident
> and wife of Whitman's literary executor

She said the first time she met him he did not feel remote from any
thing not from the people or the trees or the flowers—not from the
animals or the people or the trees—he made her feel like all things
were in space together—together in the space of all things.

This coming together to be a whole one—all the people and trees
and flowers—he made her feel like all things were in space with
them together—a flower in them to their feeling—his love was
anybody's love, a joy to any one loving very well in their living—
and his love was for all things and their mothers—his feeling of
loving for mothers—a feeling of loving, an immeasurable flowering
of words.

How a collection of words brings us together—together in a space
of all things—all the mothers and flowers and words—how we like
to see them and touch them and keep them all safe—of knowing
they are safe in their living—this collection of people and things
in their boxes—to create a space for all the people and things.

WE LEFT HOME TO COME AND MAKE OUR WAY HERE

She was skinny with giant brown eyes
and a house the same shape as mine.
The house where she did so many chores.
Such a thing that some can remember.
That day we swept droppings from the floor.

I remember her mother with a bible.
Her mother and her giant brown eyes.
And her father with his hands on my shoulders.
In her room the same shape as mine.
Such a feeling that some can remember.
A moment that passes.
A moment we save.

She remembers my mother at the front door.
Fixed in her memory a figure.
How my mother taught her to do fractions with oranges.
A way of finding themselves inside them.

To find out what the other was remembering.
Remembering a far away place.
She lives far away now from the place of this writing.
She lives a kind of new country living.
She says it's beautiful: all the mountains and rivers and trees.
Still she wishes her neighbors would be nicer.
Her neighbors in the country who ask her to tell them
why some people choose to live in ghettos.

She's far away now from the place of this writing,
but she says all the places are still very close.
She says it's not just that the pretzels taste better.
It's just the fact that it's home.

ANYTHING IS AUTOBIOGRAPHY BUT THIS WAS A CONVERSATION

What my mother said to me
about herself in other words
was that she wanted to use all the words she had
all at the same time, so that she could remember
all the words she had, and what they said,
about herself and others.

What she said to me was:

Some can see me right away, others can't.   They
                get confused or they think they
        are confused or they're not confused.
It's very, very mixed up.

                          I was in a car.
I don't think I was going anywhere I wanted to go
                so that was nice
      because I did get to some places I didn't see
and I saw them.

What she said to me in other words
was that she wanted to use all the words
she could remember that described coming and going,
all the words she had that described
how she remembered me.

What she said to me was:

              Back and forth back and forth in the kitchen
                        back and forth   in the kitchen   back to
                              school. I don't know where the school
              is   she goes   to the school of the
                    week   or school of the year
school of this score of that   I don't always get it.

              When we're going out, she's coming in
                              from being with friends.
It's good she's doing that   because I know them
                    from there more than I know them from nobody.
              I like to know them from where I know them
                              or what they said
                    or where we went.

What she said to me not in so many words
was that there were dangers she didn't have words for.

She said—

         Always sort of checking on them.   Or they're
checking on us, I should say.
              We always say come on, let's go,
    this is killing us.
        They get them   right there
             and shoot them.
   I don't know who they are   some group that travels
                    around.
         They're probably friendless.
They think they are doing the only thing people do.
              And so much
    is not that.
    And that's the part I thought you could take care of.
    You know,   for the warmth of it.

What she said to me about the one
who was to her who she was to me
was—

                She does what she wants, mother,
                      but she's not careless.
    She drove the Pontiac Bold '32.
                      They didn't go far.
I guess talking about it more than anything.   We didn't
             actually get out there and do a lot.
       We just talked about it and talked about it
    till they said we're going. So we went.
            Ocean City.   And we had that
              and that never changed.

    Even now, if we decide to go, we go
          because it's memory.

    You know   from the memory.

A DEAD ONE A ONE BEING DYING AND I AM FILLED THEN WITH COMPLETE DESOLATION

The point the phone tree starts when Patty tells me you have pneumonia when I call Karen and go back to my puzzle. The point in a puzzle when it's about choices. The point Patty calls to say they think you had a heart attack when the doctors say they'll run some tests. The point in a puzzle when it's about color. The point MaryJean calls to say you asked after me she says you asked if the door was locked she says you asked for your keys. The point in a puzzle when it's about shades. The point Ann calls and asks me to talk into the phone when I say can you hear me and I hear something like breathing and I hear something like drowning. The point in the puzzle when it's about trying out options one by one. The point Ann says we have to tell you everyone's ok she says when everyone's ok you can shut your eyes. The point Ann says you're passing when you're passing and I'm talking into the phone and saying I'm sorry you're sick and I love you. The point I don't hear you. The point I don't hear anything like breathing. The point I don't hear anything like drowning. The point we hang up and call back or stay on the phone I can't remember I was pacing and then sitting and then walking into the bedroom to tell Tasha you're dead and she says oh Susie. The point I want to tell everyone I know what has happened. The point I text Allison my mother is dead I can't speak. The point your children go over what happened when the fluid built up but you seemed verbal when they rolled you over and you seized when you aspirated when you had a cardiac event when you were in distress when everyone said you're DNR when the doctors said get the morphine when the nurses said get the family. The point I want to write everything down. The point I want everyone I know to know of this grief and don't know who to let know of this grief or how. The point I sink into the floor. The point your children go over what's going to happen. When we talk about underwear when we talk about pumps when Karen says they sell caskets at Costco when Ann says a pine box isn't as bad as you think. The point the funeral can't come soon enough. The point your children go over what's going to happen. The embalming the dressing the cosmetology the opening of the grave the liner the memorial package the obituary the spray the prayer cards the certified copies the cantor the what-to-do-if-it-rains. The point I start drinking. The point I post pictures on Facebook. The point I want everyone on Facebook to like everything I am posting on Facebook. The point I get mad at everyone on Facebook who isn't liking everything I am posting on Facebook. The point I go to work and feel sick. The point I shut my office door. The point I open it the point I shut it the point I open it again. The point co-workers start dropping by. The point co-workers start telling me about their mothers. The point co-workers start to look uncomfortable so I hug them and this makes them feel better. The point I'm standing at the back of a long line to board a train and a door opens behind me and suddenly I'm the first to board. The point I think maybe you're watching. The point I ask others if they think you could really be watching. The point I hope you aren't really watching. The point MaryJean tells me to stand at the end of a line. The point I walk away from the line and Ann brings me back when I shake hands and say thank you to the people lining up to walk down a line. The point I worry my composure may worry the people lining up to shake my hand at the end of a line. The point I see someone who is not you lying in a casket. The point I want to touch this body that is not you but feel afraid so back away. The point I step forward. The point my lips are shaking on your forehead on your forehead as hard as stone and colder. The point I sit down and hear a story about drinking blood. The point I sit down and hear a story about eating flesh. The point the story of your life gets told through stories about the deaths of others. The point I lean into your casket and worry about falling into a grave. The point everyone goes to a restaurant and the kids drink half-and-half. The point MaryJean tells me about the night your cat had kittens the night you fed the runt milk from a spoon the night the runt died. The point Ann says her daughter thinks animals can talk in heaven so when we get there we'll find out what they've been thinking all this time. The point everyone says you're with others. The point the day is over and we watch *Seinfeld*.

The point I wake up in the middle of the night and say there are no words. The point I fall back asleep and dream about a maze a maze where people disappear around corners a maze where I have to retrace my steps or else get lost. The point I get on a subway and say my mother is dead I'm getting a seat. The point everything feels radically simple. The point I go to look at the eagle the brass eagle with brass feathers in what used to be Wanamaker's the eagle where people meet up after separating. The point I tell Tasha that part of this grieving is helping others respond to my grief and she says once others lose sight of my grief all I'll be left with is grieving. The point it's a week later and I return to my puzzle. The point I'm picking up pieces and reveling in metaphor then look up and decide not to finish.

THE PLACE THAT WAS TO BE FOR A LONG TIME A HOME TO THEM

How the premise or messuage extended—how it extended along a street named for no one between streets named for men—how it extended to people in little houses—people living in little houses who are part of a history that is living—how it extended to the people who live there like Yolanda.

I told Yolanda my mother's last thoughts were of her children in her house—Yolanda's house, my mother's. She told me about seeing the house for the first time—how there were pictures of us on the wall—how she couldn't believe my mother raised eight children there—she said there weren't any holes in the walls—the doors were on all of their hinges.

She told me she wasn't psychic, but that she feels things—and when she feels things she knows to pay attention—like when she looked at the other house before this one—the one she just looked at and cried—the one she couldn't go into because some houses are empty for good reason—how she kept looking until she found this one—where she felt only goodness and care.

She said when she first got to the block there was some madness, a shooting—but it got quiet pretty soon after that—she said every place has pockets of quiet and pockets of madness—everyone knows where to go.

She told me she found things we left behind—names scribbled in closets—a broken window in the basement—so few she didn't see them at first—like the rosebush in the backyard that bloomed right after her grandmother's passing—her grandmother who had little pink roses on her casket—how she didn't see them at first, the little roses in the backyard—how she calls it Nana's rosebush now.

just ordinary talking   to talk about little things

in a house not an airlite but a shotgun or a railroad

on the street named for no one   how it extended

how it extended   into a history

that is living

ALL THE POETRY OF LIVING

A poem for David—the guardian of a house with a history and a couch—David who says we can talk about the couch as an object— an object in a house battered by cannons—a couch worth a lot of money—or we can talk about the man who made it—a man named Affleck, an objector—to approach an object by its subject the objector is interpretation—Affleck the Quaker, the unrestrained maker—a man branded a traitor and sent to a Guantanamo of his time—a history to turn over in the mind—to chew—the Chew house a mansion made from slave labor—a poem for David who says people come here just to see the couch—David who says the things we agree on are the least meaningful.

A poem for Mary who says we are all trying to find our place on the map—Mary and her siblings who were the only white children at their school—a school that bussed its black students far away— Mary whose father wondered why the buses didn't bring white children from far away to the school nearby but no one would answer his question.

A poem for Joe who works across the street from a hollow once a quarry—who tells me to go to the Cricket Club—who tells me after the French won the Davis at the Cricket Club they needed a place to defend their title so they had to build Roland Garros—Joe who says they built Roland Garros because of what happened in Germantown—Joe who says you can't leave that out.

A poem for Kia who says living inside a place means living outside of others, like the Cricket Club on one side and the projects on the other—who tells me Germantown isn't North Philly and it's not Mt. Airy either.

A poem for Simone who says there's the experience of living in a place and the mythology of living in a place—Simone who gives me the word boxwood.

A poem for Gertrude whose father-in-law ran the hearth at Midvale Steel—where the unskilled could always find work—Midvale Steel and its little death wagon.

A poem for Tom riding his bike past the bus stop where Mrs. Sereni's heart stopped—a poem for Mrs. Sereni whose marble table had a fossil in it.

A poem for Stan writing a poem inspired by Dlugos while biking by Dlugos' house every day without knowing it.

A poem for Terri reading poems in the park—poems about white men fighting black men driving trolleys—about trolleys full of bayonets during wartime—bayonets to break a hate strike—and a woman in the park shouting, I remember—a woman in Vernon Park shouting, I'm an elephant.

A poem about taking pictures on a roof near a train station—pictures of a church dome and a water tower in the shape of a Vicks VapoRub tub—a poem about coming down from the roof and the men on the corner asking us what we were taking pictures of—a poem about surveys and surveillance.

A poem about the surveillance camera that captured Carlesha's abduction off the street—and the LoJack inside her captor's car— the tracker the car dealer put in without the man's knowledge— the man with bad credit and a knife who took Carlesha as far as Maryland before the police could track them down.

A poem for Edi who shares her name with a woman whose husband was killed at a train station—a woman who sued the city because they knew the station was dangerous—a poem about meeting Edi to see if she had a husband—about meeting Edi and this not coming up.

A poem for Erica whose daughter's teacher screamed all day long—Erica who told her teachert that 38 kids to a class isn't right but screaming isn't either so quit it and she did.

A poem for Sam who handed me boxes full of newspapers from the '70s—boxes full of fighting—fighting about cops and gas prices and nuclear power—fighting about supermarkets leaving and fast food moving in.

A poem for Mark who reads every scrap of paper about a family in the archives—who says history only gets bigger as you make your way through all the boxes.

A poem for Christopher Durang the playwright whose grandfather built the church that was the beginning of this writing—Durang who tells me he has nostalgic feelings about the looks of churches and some of the priests and nuns and some of the teachings and the orderliness of it all.

A poem for Renny and plastic barrettes—the barrettes he calls little girls, 7 and 8, who lose their flowers everyday—plastic barrettes on a sidewalk—trash he arranges and frames—so much trash he decided to pick it up himself—to pick it up and paint it and put it back down again—a poem for Renny painting all the trash gold—all the bottles, the vials, and the poop—a poem about spray painting all the poop gold—until they showed up in their army of trucks—to take all the gold away.

A poem for Vashti who turned her house into an art gallery—a gallery to visit for no more than 15 minutes because eviction is urgent.

A poem for Ingrid who never met a homeowner who didn't love their home.

A poem for YahNe who invites me to her house to read her memoir—her memories of the man she loved who was a liar—who didn't throw her down the stairs even though his word was his bond.

A poem for Lenny who's been inside Sun Ra's house—who tells me they think Ra is alive—a poem for Lenny who wrote this place isn't haunted, what happened happened, it won't happen again.

A poem for Marshall all red sequins and a sax—Marshall with his hands high with a shake—arms like a wrench singing maybe tomorrow the sun will come.

A poem for Howard—who used to roller skate who was a boy scout who learned a trade—who went from potman to dishwasher—who's missing teeth—who rolled the rounds and skirted the tables—who likes to drink—who says he cleans up Germantown to make it look like Chestnut Hill—who says I need a resume, I don't know how to make a resume, who says I need help with that.

A poem for Tieshka telling me there are two sides to every story like a park where you can get everything you never wanted—or a mural of a park inside a park—with vines both real and imagined—

vines that repeat like a drum like concrete—a poem about being all caught up in it, the vines of this place, this repeating.

EPILOGUE

IT WAS MY DESIGN TO EXPLAIN (PART 2)

In 1978, a new library opened in the neighborhood. In the center of the children's section was an enormous bookcase in the shape of a dragon. Near the dragon was an alcove of biographies. I remember taking one out on Benjamin Franklin and signing my name on a card in the back.

Franklin gets credited for creating the first library in America. He called it his first project of a public nature. He was aided by his mentor James Logan who lived in an estate in Nicetown, just past Wayne Junction. Logan's house, called Stenton, is considered one of the best-preserved historic buildings in Philadelphia. It's a squat, boxy house made of brick. During the Battle of Germantown, a woman named Dinah who was once a slave, or might have still been a slave, saved the house from British soldiers who tried to burn it down.

As the course of this writing moved beyond little windows on the internet and onto train lines and streets inscribed to memory, my brother Tom let me stay with him when I came to visit. He and his family live in Mt. Airy, a largely middle-class, racially diverse neighborhood next to Germantown, where people who know a little bit about Philadelphia think I'm from when I tell them I'm from Germantown. Tom and I rode his tandem from Mt. Airy to

Stenton by riding down Wayne Avenue, named after the general, and past the train station named after him too.

I had never been to Stenton before, or Nicetown, the neighborhood with a name some might consider ironic. A year or so after our visit, a co-worker told me about growing up in Nicetown. He told me about a neighbor who shot her husband after he left their house carrying a TV. He told me when the cops outlined the body in chalk, they drew a little TV under the arm.

The caretaker at Stenton told us Logan told Franklin which books to buy for his library. Logan, an expert on so many things.

Before the beginning of this writing, it had been years since I had used a library. I had forgotten how part of using a library is walking down a corridor, or up a flight of stairs, or waiting for a book to come from somewhere else. How part of using a library is not getting an answer right away.

It's a place where in the walking and the waiting, I thought about this writing.

A place to think about walking closer to this writing.

To walk around it while thinking it through.

Behind the library in Germantown there's a small street tucked behind another street, like a secret alcove, named Armat. The smaller street is lined with quaint, dollhouse-like houses, each one different from the next. I couldn't find any architectural terms to describe them. Someone told me they are of the Germantown vernacular.

In 1976, the houses on the little street were converted into stores and renamed Maplewood Mall. As a child, I got my hair cut on the mall. One time the hairdresser got distracted while drying my hair. I sat silently, scalp burning, certain that at any point she would move the nozzle away.

Trust in authority a kind of faith.

Today, many of the properties on the mall are vacant, but a few are rented or have stores — the music studio, a vitamin shop, the window where Nick canes chairs — Nick, who says chairs lose their memory but a damp cloth restores. A weeping willow shades the center of the block. Orange bollards separate the mall's narrow stone roadway from the sidewalk and serve as seats or drums for children walking by.

A happy, hollow sound.

Throughout the course of this writing, I found myself walking through the mall over and over. To walk around it while thinking it through. Past the orange drum-seats, the weeping willow, the faded kiosk listing shops no longer there. And across the street, the bus stop, where I waited each day after school. The bus stop on the corner where most white kids took the bus one way, and I took it the other.

And in my walking through the mall throughout the course of this writing, I came to see the mall not as a border or a lost place or a secret, but as a real place where people like to gather.

Where they gather and invite me inside.

Where they invite me inside where they gather in a place that is imperfect and living.

On one end of the mall is an art gallery called iMPeRFeCT, opened just before the beginning of this writing. In my first conversation with Tieshka Smith, a local photographer, she told me about a show she was staging at the gallery. She told me there were two sides to Germantown, the historic one and the real one and her show was about the latter, the one where people aren't stressing about organic carrots. In my first conversation with Tieshka, she asked me to read poems at her opening, an offer so generous I couldn't refuse.

To be reading about this place and its people with the people who live in this place.

As the buses go by one way and then the other.

To be worried about doing a place justice.

To have worries fade as the sun set around our voices.

As applause bounced off the bollards, our little drum-seats.

To read poems about this place with its people. And to hear poems about Obama and Mondays and home. Songs of Tupac and Tubman and love.

It was an old place and entirely new.

And afterwards we milled about and talked. And some of us drank and some of us smoked and some of us laughed or listened or shrugged. People in a place that is living. How we talked about schools and family the weather. People talking and sitting and thinking. Walking and fighting and waiting. Singing and nodding and listening. Being whole beings in our living. How the moon was bright above us and I said my god what a beautiful night.

I've been thinking that this writing moves like a spiral.

Moving from afar to close in or back out.

To touch down in places hard to navigate.

To think through it by walking it through.

Long before the beginning of this writing, I had retreated from this place. Retreat, a word of war.

I had moved away for college to go to a school attended over-whelmingly by wealthy, white people who frequently told me they were from Detroit or some other city they actually lived outside of. I was there because I got good grades or applied early. Applied early or got good funding. I remember getting some funding from a scholarship at my high school. A prize the girls at high school said was only for white girls. I don't know if that was true.

After leaving for college, I lived in Germantown only once more, for the summer after my freshman year. I remember thinking how much smaller the small house had become. How much dimmer the unlit train station. How peculiar it seemed that my mother wedged a chair under the cellar door at night.

To see something the way one's been seeing it and then seeing it again somehow new.

Elijah Anderson describes poor neighborhoods as "often dangerous and highly stressful for [their] residents, at times imperceptibly so. It is sometimes not until a person moves or travels away from such a place that he or she comes to appreciate the level of relaxation missed in the inner-city neighborhood."

Anderson uses Germantown Avenue as a framing device in his book, *Code of the Street*. The avenue cuts through the full spectrum of Philadelphia's economic and racial diversity. A great road. And while the bulk of his study is concerned with people living in neighborhoods poorer or labeled more dangerous than German-town, where the stresses he describes disproportionately impact people of color, I felt an affinity with Anderson's words.

How I had never thought twice about my mother's locking up rituals until I moved away. Until I moved away to apartments with windows wide open and streets full of people after dark. That sense of relaxation after moving. How I wanted to hold on to that feeling.

Throughout my adult life, when I tell people where I grew up they respond with various levels of disbelief. Like the people who tell me they love Germantown and then go on to describe Mt. Airy or Chestnut Hill where more wealthy or white people live. Or the ones who suggest my background is so unusual, I must have so many stories to tell. Or the man who insisted I tell him the cross streets of the house I grew up in. Or the woman who said, you don't have any hood in you.

How should I prove my impossible origins? One place to begin is with a sense of threat. Cats, mouths heavy with birds, at the door.

Out the back door of the house I grew up in, past the backyard where I caught lightning bugs in summer, was Larry's house. The one he lived in with his brothers. The brothers who played music all night. Summer nights full of thumping. My mother called them drug dealers. I don't know if that was true. One time one of them lifted me up right over his head. I remember seeing my legs kicking while he laughed.

Out the front door of the house I grew up in was a man who was always watching me. He was always naked. In a doorway, on his porch, in an alley, in the summer, in the winter, he'd be watching, he'd be naked. A man who I—years later as an adult—imagined could suddenly appear wherever I was living. Something I imagined was quite possible until I realized it was never me he wanted, but children. To realize how many years I had thought there was something in me that caused his behavior. A moment like a lightning bolt jolting me to life.

And inside the front door and the back door of the house I grew up in was my brother, not the one who lives in Mt. Airy, but the other one, the sick one, with no teeth. The one who got his teeth knocked out at Christmas. Who got his teeth knocked out at Christmas by Larry's brothers. How he came home drunk and bleeding, cursing out our neighbors on Christmas.

Christmas always so special at the church.

A memory of frankincense and echoes.

My brother who I wanted to give no place to in this writing but who found a place in this writing after a conversation. A conversation I had with a co-worker. My white co-worker who grew up in Nicetown, a predominately black neighborhood. A man I reached out to because his background was so unusual, I thought he must have so many stories to tell.

And how he told me about his father in the basement, listening to Morse code after drinking. How his father blamed his wife's death on his son's birth. Stories full of repeating.

The familiar repeating of drinking and screaming.

Pockets of madness.

Pockets of quiet.

Everyone knows where to go.

That sense of relaxation after moving away. How I wanted to hold on to that feeling.

The things we hold on to till we can't carry them any more.

Like the notion of my impossible origins.

How they were never impossible at all.

How I came to see this as I came to know a place and its people.

This place I am a part of   and apart from
that is a part of me.

This place where I lived with so many people I didn't look like,
but my living was circumscribed mostly by those I did.

The white lines of history all around me:

coveting the houses of colonizers

kneeling before Irish saints

working illegally in a legal drug trade.

How it's taken me a while to see this.

How I needed to listen in order to see.

So many stories I have come to be hearing. About this place where
I lived so much of my living. A kind of living unlike many others.
Like Nzadi's father who set pins in the bowling alley. A job my
uncle had once, too. The bowling alley next to the dining hall
where Nzadi's father wasn't allowed to sit down. Or the depart-
ment store where her mother bought shoes. The store where my
father bought me the mauve dress I'd wear to his funeral. How the
clerk made Nzadi's mother put a piece of paper inside the shoes
she wanted to try on.

How I came to see

how much more I need always to be listening

to you, the place of this writing,

and you, the people of this place

                    and all the history

we are a part of   that is a part of us,

                              the

                  we

of incense and boxwood and brick

      pride and bullets and prayer

            wisteria and helicopters and figs

turtles and burkas and hacks

      block captains raccoons and lilies

            pianos and hydrants and sirens

the barber the yarn bomb the shrine

      the whosoever the just-like-that braids

            the shut-ins the playground the steeple

the sugar shack the in-and-out the charm

      in a half-house or trilling bell passage

            all the people and times all combined.

The layers that break through every surface

                of us.   The we

      who aren't broken   who
aren't easy.

We

        of strong bones

   I can't end us.

We

   who are always

   beginning.

ACKNOWLEDGMENTS

Versions of poems in this book have appeared in: *The Brooklyn Rail, Capitalism Nature Socialism, Elderly, Eleven Eleven, EOAGH, Epiphany Magazine, Horseless Review, The Offing, ONandOnScreen, The Philadelphia Review of Books, Talking Writing, West Wind Review, Where Eagles Dare,* and in a limited edition chapbook produced by Cannot Exist.

I am forever indebted to everyone who talked to me about their experiences of, and insights into, Germantown—especially those who currently live there. Special thanks to: Tamara Anderson, Alex Bartlett, Ann Beatus, Lenny Belasco, Joe and Rita Beyer, Yolanda Booker, Mark Bower, Kim Broadbent, Rocio Cabello, Edi Montijo Chapman, Peter Cherbas, Sydney Coffin, Kia Connelly-Baker, Karie Diethorn, Aine and Emaleigh Doley, Vashti DuBois, Walter Dunston, Ed Feldman, Pat Ganley, Gerry and Lorraine Givnish, Pat Harkins, Chris Higgins, Howard, Kim Jackson, James Johnson IV, Monique Jones, Nzadi Keita, Jeanne King, Erika Kitzmiller, Ali Landers, Christine Landers, Jean Landers, Karen Landers, Sue (Witter) Landers, Tom Landers, Adam Levine, Terri Lyons, Susan Mangan, Regina McDermott, Virginia Mechling, Gina Michaels, Renny Molenaar, Mary Morrow-Farrell, YahNe Ndgo, MaryJean O'Byrne, Gerald Parker, Paula Paul, John Phillips, Marlene Pryor, Ethel Rackin, Raymond Raybold, Gary Reed, Mark Anthony Robinson, Ingrid Shepherd, Father Eugene Sheridan, Erica Siate, Michael Silverstein, Karen Singer, Karen Smith, Tieshka Smith, Jeff Templeton, Robyn Tevah, Tiptoe, Gertrude Walsh, Ken Weinstein, Allison Weiss, Simone White, Bryan Willette, Yolanda Wisher, Rachael Woldoff, and David Young.

Thanks, also, to my closest readers and the best editors anyone could ever hope for: Natasha Dwyer, Allison Cobb, James Sherry, and Brandon Brown.

IMAGE CREDITS

Special thanks to C.E. Putnam and Praveen Vajpeyi who helped me select and arrange the images in this book.

Cover artwork: Ann Landers Beatus

Page 11. Franklin-Stein collage by Jen Coleman.

Page 15. My parents at the altar of St. Francis of Assisi on their wedding day, May 22, 1954. Photo courtesy of the author.

Page 18. Beyer Stained Glass Studio, rear entry on Keyser Street between Wyneva and Logan, 2013. Photo by the author.

Page 19. Artifacts from my childhood home, 2014. Photo by the author.

Page 20. St. Francis of Assisi farewell Mass, June 24, 2012. Photo by Theresa Stigale for Hidden City Philadelphia.

Page 21. Cover of 1983 *Zeit Magazin*, taken at Cliveden in 2012. Photo by the author.

Page 22. Hood Cemetery, corner of Germantown Avenue and Logan Street, 2012. Photo by Ethan Fugate.

Page 24. Screenshot of Google street view, corner of Wyneva Street and Wayne Avenue, 2012.

Page 27. Map detail, taken in the archive of the Philadelphia Streets Department, 2012. Photo by the author.

Page 73. Author photo, circa 1975.

Page 86. Corner of Wayne Avenue and Berkley Street, taken from the roof of the Max Levy building, 2012. Photo by the author.

Page 86. Inside Wayne Mills, the last remaining factory in operation in the Wayne Junction Historical District, 2012. Photo by the author.

Page 87. Venturi, Scott Brown, and Associates' "ghost structure" at Franklin Court, where Franklin's house once stood, Old City, Philadelphia, 2013. Photo by the author.

Page 87. The phone bank in the original Benjamin Franklin Underground Museum. Photo by C.E. Putnam.

Page 88. The Winston Building in Center City, Philadelphia where my father worked for 25 years before the union was busted (now luxury lofts), 2013. Photo by the author.

Page 89. The letter my father wrote me two days before he died. Photo by the author.

Page 90. My mother and father, with her parents, at their wedding reception outside Alden Park, 1954. Photo courtesy of the author.

Page 90. Alden Park, 2012. Photo by the author.

Page 91. Remaining structures at Rittenhousetown, the first paper mill in the United States, 2012. Photo by the author.

Page 91. A "half-house" on Wayne Avenue near Queen Lane, 2014. Photo by the author.

Page 92. Home Owners' Loan Corporation "security map" of Philadelphia, 1936. Retrieved from Amy Hillier's website "Redlining in Philadelphia," http://nis.cml.upenn.edu/redlining.

Page 93. Map of Philadelphia Catholic Parishes (1949) courtesy of Beyer Studio.

Page 94. Rocio Cabello and Renny Molenaar, with their sons, Giza and Cory. Photographed July 2013 by Tieshka Smith.

Page 94. Tieshka Smith (self-portrait). Photographed November 2014.

Page 95. Allison Weiss. Photographed September 2012 by Tieshka Smith.

Page 95. Aine and Emaleigh Doley on Rockland Street. Photographed by Neal Santos.

Page 97. Re-imagine Maplewood Mall Festival 2014. Photo by the author.

Page 104. Glass negative of Beautiful Witch, taken at the Fairmount Parks Commission archives, 2012. Photo by the author.

Page 111. My mother and me, outside Philadelphia High School for Girls, 1989. Photo courtesy of the author.

Page 117. The couch at Cliveden, 2012. Photo by the author.

Page 121. "Howard protests." Photographed July 2012 near Maplewood Mall by Tieshka Smith.

Page 123. Artist rendering of the Germantown mural at 310 W. Chelten Avenue. Courtesy of muralist Jon Laidacker.

Page 125. Dragon bookshelf, designed by Stewart Paul, at the Joseph Coleman Northwest Regional Library, 2012. Photo by the author.

Page 126. Stenton, 4601 N. 18th Street, 2012. Photo by the author.

Page 127. Maplewood Mall, 2013. Photo by the author.

Page 129. Osiris Wildfire and Tiptoe. Photographed July 2013 at iMPeRFeCT Gallery by Tieshka Smith.

Page 130. Street sign near Wayne Junction, 2012. Photo by the author.

BIBLIOGRAPHY

Every title in *Franklinstein* is a direct quote from *The Autobiography of Benjamin Franklin* or *The Making of Americans*. In addition to drawing from those texts for language and inspiration, each of the following sources informed my writing in some way. I am grateful for these creators and their creations.

Texts
Ali, Kazim. *Bright Felon: Autobiography and Cities*. Middletown: Wesleyan University Press, 2009.

Anderson, Elijah. *Code of the Street*. New York: W.W. Norton, 2000.

Aristotle. *Poetics*. Project Gutenberg, 1999.

Asante, MK. *Buck*. New York: Spiegel & Grau, 2013.

Bacon, Edmund. *Design of Cities*. New York: Viking Press, 1967.

Ballard, Allen. *One More Day's Journey: The Story of a Family and a People*. New York: McGraw-Hill, 1984.

Bennett, Jacob A. *Wysihicken [sic]*. Towson: Furniture Press, 2014.

Bergman, Luke. *Getting Ghost: Two Young Lives and the Struggle for the Soul of an American City*. Ann Arbor: University of Michigan Press, 2010.

Bergvall, Caroline. *Drift*. Brooklyn: Nightboat Books, 2014.

Bower, Mark Arnold. *Loudoun, Germantown, Philadelphia: Country House of the Armat Family: The Years 1801-1835* (Masters Thesis). University of Pennsylvania, 1984.

Brainard, Joe. *I Remember*. New York: Granary Books, 2001.

Brown, Brandon. *Top 40*. New York: Roof Books, 2014.

Bryant, Tisa. *Tzimmes*. San Francisco: A+bend Press, 2000.

Butler, Octavia. *Parable of the Sower*. New York: Four Walls Eight Windows, 1993.

_____ *Parable of the Talents*. New York: Seven Stories Press, 1998.

Carson, Anne. *Autobiography of Red*. New York: Knopf, 1998.

Clemens, Colleen. *Philadelphia Reflections*. Charleston: History Press, 2011.

Cole, Teju. *Open City*. New York: Random House, 2011.

Collins, Martha. *Blue Front*. St. Paul: Graywolf Press, 2006.

Conrad, CA. *A Beautiful Marsupial Afternoon*. Seattle: Wave Books, 2012.

Conrad, CA and Frank Sherlock. *The City Real & Imagined*. Queens: Factory School, 2010.

Coultas, Brenda. *The Bowery Project*. San Francisco: Leroy Press, 2003.

_____ *The Tatters*. Middletown: Wesleyan University Press, 2014.

Countryman, Matthew. *Up South*. Philadelphia: University of Pennsylvania Press, 2006.

de Angeli, Marguerite. *Bright April*. Garden City: Doubleday, 1946.

Deford, Frank. *Big Bill Tilden: The Triumphs and the Tragedy*. New York: Simon & Schuster, 1976.

Durang, Christopher. *Marriage of Bette and Boo*. New York: Dramatists Play Service, 1985.

139

_____ *Sister Mary Ignatius Explains It All For You*. New York: Dramatists Play
  Service, 1982.

Eckes, Ryan. *Old News*. Towson: Furniture Press Books, 2011.

Farnsworth, Jean M., Carmen R. Croce and Joseph F. Chorpenning. *Stained
  Glass in Catholic Philadelphia*. Philadelphia: Saint Joseph's University
  Press, 2002.

Franklin, Benjamin. *The Autobiography of Benjamin Franklin*. New York:
  Dover Publications, 1996.

Greiff, Constance M. *Independence: The Creation of a National Park*.
  Philadelphia: University of Pennsylvania Press, 1987.

Hagen, Carrie. *We Is Got Him: The Kidnapping That Changed America*. New
  York: Overlook Press, 2011.

Harryman, Carla. *Baby*. New York: Adventures in Poetry, 2005.

_____ *Memory Play*. Oakland: O Books, 1994.

Hejinian, Lyn. *My Life*. Los Angeles: Sun & Moon Press, 1987.

Heller, Gregory. *Ed Bacon: Planning, Politics, and the Building of Modern
  Philadelphia*. Philadelphia: University of Pennsylvania Press, 2013.

Hocker, Edward. *Germantown 1683-1933*. Philadelphia: self-published, 1933.

Howe, Susan. *Spontaneous Particulars*. New York: New Directions, 2014.

Hunt, Marsha. *Free*. New York: Dutton, 1993.

Johnson, Barbara. "My Monster/My Self." *Diacritics*, 12 (Summer 1992), 2-10.

Jones, Solomon. *Dead Man's Wife*. New York: Minotaur Books, 2012.

Kapil, Bhanu. *Incubator: A Space for Monsters*. New York: Leon Works, 2006.

Karr, Mary, *Lit: A Memoir*. New York: Harper, 2009.

Kaufman, Ned. *Place, Race, and Story*. New York: Routledge, 2009.

Keita, Nzadi Zimele. *Birthmarks*. Troy: Nightshade Press, 1993.

Kenny, Kevin. *Peaceable Kingdom Lost: The Paxton Boys and the Destruction
  of William Penn's Holy Experiment*. New York: Oxford University Press,
  2009.

Kephart, Beth. *Flow*. Philadelphia: Temple University Press, 2007.

Keyser, Naaman. *History of Old Germantown*. Philadelphia: H.F. McCann,
  1907.

Laymon, Kiese. *Long Division*. Chicago: Bolden, 2013.

Lepore, Jill. *Book of Ages: The Life and Opinions of Jane Franklin*. New York:
  Knopf, 2013.

Lippard, George. *Battle-Day of Germantown*. Philadelphia: Diller, 1843.

Lippard, George and David S. Reynolds, ed. *Prophet of Protest: Writings of an
  American Radical, 1822–1854*. New York: P. Lang, 1986.

Lopez, Claude-Anne. *My Life with Benjamin Franklin*. New Haven: Yale
  University Press, 2000.

Lyons, Jonathan. *The Society for Useful Knowledge: How Benjamin Franklin
  and Friends Brought the Enlightenment to America*. New York: Bloomsbury
  Press, 2013.

Magi, Jill. *Labor*. Brooklyn: Nightboat Books, 2014.

Mason, Randall. *The Once and Future New York*. Minneapolis: University of
  Minnesota Press, 2009.

Massey, Joseph. *To Keep Time*. Richmond: Omnidawn, 2014.

Matero, Frank G., "Ben's House: Designing History at Franklin Court, Philadelphia." *Archaeological Institute of America* (May 2010).

Mathis, Ayana. *The Twelve Tribes of Hattie*. New York: Knopf, 2012.

McGreevy, John. *Parish Boundaries: The Catholic Encounter with Race in the Twentieth-Century Urban North*. Chicago: University of Chicago Press, 1996.

Medsger, Betty. *The Burglary: The Discovery of J. Edgar Hoover's Secret FBI*. New York: Knopf, 2014.

Miegs, Mary. *The Box-Closet*. Toronto: Talonbooks, 1987.

Mullen, Harryette. *Urban Tumbleweed: Notes from a Tanka Diary*. Minneapolis: Graywolf Press, 2013.

Niedecker, Lorine. *Paean to Place*. Milwaukee: Woodland Pattern, 2003.

Norris, Kathleen. *Virgin of Bennington*. New York: Riverhead Books, 2001.

Notley, Alice. *Close to Me & Closer*. Oakland: O Books, 1995.

_____ *Descent of Alette*. New York: Penguin, 1996.

_____ *Mystery of Small Houses*. New York: Penguin, 1998.

Palm, Kristin. *The Straits*. Long Beach: Palm Press, 2008.

Perkiss, Abigail. *Racing the City: Intentional Integration and the Pursuit of Racial Justice in Post-WWII America* (Masters Thesis). Temple University, 2010.

Pinter, Harold. *No Man's Land*. New York: Grove Press, 1975.

Popkin, Nathaniel. *The Possible City: Exercises in Dreaming Philadelphia*. Philadelphia: Camino Books, 2008.

_____ *Song of the City*. New York: Four Walls Eight Windows, 2002.

Ra, Sun. *This Planet is Doomed*. New York: Kicks Books, 2011.

Rankine, Claudia. *Citizen*. Minneapolis: Graywolf Press, 2014.

_____ *Don't Let Me Be Lonely*. Saint Paul: Graywolf Press, 2004.

Reinarman, Craig and Harry G. Levine, eds. *Crack in America: Demon Drugs and Social Justice*. Berkeley: University of California Press, 1997.

Retallack, Joan. *The Poethical Wager*. Berkeley: University of California Press, 2003.

Sanchez, Sonia. *Morning Haiku*. Boston: Beacon Press, 2010.

Sand, Kaia. *Remember to Wave*. Kane'ohe: Tinfish Press, 2010.

Scalapino, Leslie. *Zither & Autobiography*. Middletown: Wesleyan University Press, 2003.

Scott, Jonathan. *The Woman in the Wilderness*. Coatesville: Middleton Books, 2005.

Scranton, Philip and Walter Licht. *Work Sights: Industrial Philadelphia, 1890-1950*. Philadelphia: Temple University Press, 1986.

Sebald, W.G. *The Emigrants*. New York: New Directions, 1996.

Seley, John, "Research on Conflict in Locational Decisions: Participation in Urbal Renewal: The Germantown Case and Julian Wolpert." (1971) (Full citation not available.)

Shakur, Assata. *Assata: An Autobiography*. Chicago: L. Hill, 1987.

Shelley, Mary. *Frankenstein*. New York: Dover Publications, 1994.

Sherlock, Frank. *Neighbor Ballads*. Philadelphia: Albion Books, 2014.

Sikelianos, Eleni. *The Loving Detail of the Living & the Dead*. Minneapolis: Coffee House Press, 2013.

_____*You Animal Machine (The Golden Greek)*. Minneapolis: Coffee House Press, 2014.

Soto Román, Carlos. *The Exit Strategy*. Brooklyn: Belladonna, 2014.

Spahr, Juliana. *This Connection of Everyone with Lungs*. Berkeley: University of California Press, 2005.

_____ *The Transformation*. Berkeley: Atelos, 2007.

Spahr, Juliana and David Buuck. *Army of Lovers*. San Francisco: City Lights, 2013.

Spahr, Juliana and Jena Osman, eds. *Chain #7: Memoir Antimemoir*. Honolulu: University of Hawaii, 2000.

Stein, Gertrude. *Everybody's Autobiography*. New York: Cooper Square Publishers, 1971.

_____ *The Making of Americans*. Normal: Dalkey Archive Press, 2009.

Strauss, Zoe. *Ten Years*. New Haven: Yale University Press, 2012.

Sugrue, Thomas. *Origins of the Urban Crisis: Race and Inequality in Postwar Detroit*. Princeton: Princeton University Press, 1996.

Szymaszek, Stacy. *Journal of Ugly Sites & Other Journals*. New York: Fence Books, 2015.

Taylor, Tess. *The Forage House*. Pasadena: Red Hen Press, 2013.

Thompson, Ahmir "Questlove". *Mo' Meta Blues, The World According to Questlove*. New York: Grand Central Publishing, 2013.

Thorson, Maureen. *My Resignation*. Bristol: Shearsman Books, 2014.

Tinkcom, Harry B. and Margaret B. *Historic Germantown: From the Founding to the Early 19th Century*. Philadelphia: American Philosophical Society, 1955.

Tyree, Omar. *Flyy Girl*. New York: Simon & Schuster, 1996.

Van Doren, Carl. *Benjamin Franklin*. New York: Viking Press, 1938.

Wagner, Catherine. *My New Job*. New York: Fence Books, 2009.

Ward, Dana. *The Crisis of Infinite Worlds*. New York: Futurepoem, 2013.

_____ *Some Other Deaths of Bas Jan Ader*. Northampton: Flowers & Cream, 2013.

Ward, Jesmyn. *Men We Reaped*. New York: Bloomsbury, 2013.

White, Simone. *Unrest*. Brooklyn: Ugly Duckling Presse, 2013.

Wilkerson, Isabel. *The Warmth of Other Suns: The Epic Story of America's Great Migration*. New York: Random House, 2010.

Wisher, Yolanda. *Monk Wears an Afro*. New York: Hanging Loose Press, 2014.

Woldoff, Rachael A. *White Flight/Black Flight: The Dynamics of Racial Change in an American Neighborhood*. Ithaca: Cornell University Press, 2011.

Wolf, Edwin. *Philadelphia: Portrait of an American City*. Harrisburg: Stackpole Books, 1975.

Wolfinger, James. *Philadelphia Divided: Race and Politics in the City of Brotherly Love*. Chapel Hill: University of North Carolina Press, 2007.

Wright, C.D. *One Big Self: An Investigation*. Port Townsend: Copper Canyon Press, 2007.

Young, David. *The Battles of Germantown: Public History and Preservation in America's Most Historic Neighborhood During the Twentieth Century* (Dissertation). Ohio State University, 2009.

Young, Stephanie. *Ursula or University*. San Francisco: Krupskaya, 2013.

Zambreno, Kate. *Heroines*. Los Angeles: Semiotext(e), 2012.

Zucker, Rachel. *The Pedestrians*. Seattle: Wave Books, 2014.

Video

"Faith on the Avenue." YouTube video, 32:49. Posted by "LTSP Communications." April 29, 2014. https://youtu.be/RaIbK5ZtAbk.

Germantown Boys. A documentary by Bianca Swift, 2012.

The House I Live In. A documentary by Eugene Jarecki, 2012.

"Journeys of Promise." YouTube video, 29:58. Posted by "John Beatty." January 3, 2012. https://youtu.be/MEmZ32o-NDw.

Let the Fire Burn. A documentary by Jason Osder, 2013.

Night Catches Us. Written and directed by Tanya Hamilton, 2010.

Philadelphia: The Great Experiment. "The Fight (1965-1978)." Created and produced by Sam Katz, 2013.

"Pipes of Peace: Rufus Harley." YouTube video, 7:41. Posted by "Jazz City-TV." March 27, 2008. https://youtu.be/zeAsSgPBmO0.

Prep School Negro. A documentary by Andre Lee, 2012.

Sun Ra: A Joyful Noise. A documentary by Robert Mugge, 1980.

We Could Be King. A documentary by Judd Ehrlich, 2014.

"Wissahickon." YouTube video, 20:04. Posted by "Ben Hyclak." May 18, 2013. https://youtu.be/3vGhn59lK1o.

- Germantown is a part of her → not "her" place
- P. 38 → the process!!
  ↳ an experiment that didn't work
- Ben Franklin's Autobiography
- Locations ≥ Memories
- Not the poem she set out to write
- P.140 "my Life" connection
- Documentary Poem, Realism
- P24 the internet, repetition
- Structure → past ≥ present
- Memories and History
- Streets named for no one
- "Don't shoot we can't breathe"
- P. 97 → conversation
- Through eyes of other people
- P.108 interlude poem about Mom
- Epologe → prose w lil poems